ANGLING SKETCHES

ANGLING SKETCHES

~ 1891 Version ~

ANDREW LANG

Edited by
George Messo

R·H·B

First published in England as *Angling Sketches,* by Longmans, Green, and Co. in 1891
This edition published 2014 by Red Hand Books

RED HAND BOOKS
Old Bath Road, London SL3 0NS
1618 Yishan Road, Minhang District, 201103 Shanghai
150th Avenue, Springfield Gardens, 11413 New York
Şerifali Mahallesi, Umraniye 34775 Istanbul
Cross Road A, Andheri, 400093 Mumbai

www.rhbks.com

Sporting Classics No. 2

ISBN: 978-0-9575977-5-4 (Paperback)

Printed and bound in the United Kingdom.

TO MRS HERBERT HILLS

'NO FISHER
BUT A WELL-WISHER
TO THE GAME'

IN MEMORY OF PLEASANT DAYS
AT CORBY

CONTENTS

~

THE CONFESSIONS OF A DUFFER	9
A BORDER BOYHOOD	16
LOCH AWE	35
LOCH-FISHING	55
LOCH LEVEN	67
THE BLOODY DOCTOR	76
THE LADY OR THE SALMON?	87
A TWEEDSIDE SKETCH	97
THE DOUBLE ALIBI	114
Editor's Afterword	140

THE CONFESSIONS OF A DUFFER

~

These papers do not boast of great sport. They are truthful, not like the tales some fishers tell. They should appeal to many sympathies. There is no false modesty in the confidence with which I esteem myself a duffer, at fishing. Some men are born duffers; others, unlike persons of genius, become so by an infinite capacity for not taking pains. Others, again, among whom I would rank myself, combine both these elements of incompetence. Nature, that made me enthusiastically fond of fishing, gave me thumbs for fingers, short-sighted eyes, indolence, carelessness, and a temper which (usually sweet and angelic) is goaded to madness by the laws of matter and of gravitation. For example: when another man is caught up in a branch he disengages his fly; I jerk at it till something breaks. As for carelessness, in boyhood I fished, by preference, with doubtful gut and knots ill-tied; it made the risk greater, and increased the excitement if one did hook a trout. I can't keep a fly-book. I stuff the flies into my pockets at random, or stick them into the leaves of a novel, or bestow them in the lining of my hat or the case of my rods. Never, till 1890, in all my days did I possess a landing-net. If

I can drag a fish up a bank, or over the gravel, well; if not, he goes on his way rejoicing. On the Test I thought it seemly to carry a landing-net. It had a hinge, and doubled up. I put the handle through a button-hole of my coat: I saw a big fish rising, I put a dry fly over him; the idiot took it. Up stream he ran, then down stream, then he yielded to the rod and came near me. I tried to unship my landing-net from my button-hole. Vain labour! I twisted and turned the handle, it would not budge. Finally, I stooped, and attempted to ladle the trout out with the short net; but he broke the gut, and went off. A landing-net is a tedious thing to carry, so is a creel, and a creel is, to me, a superfluity. There is never anything to put in it. If I do catch a trout, I lay him under a big stone, cover him with leaves, and never find him again. I often break my top joint; so, as I never carry string, I splice it with a bit of the line, which I bite off, for I really cannot be troubled with scissors and I always lose my knife. When a phantom minnow sticks in my clothes, I snap the gut off, and put on another, so that when I reach home I look as if a shoal of fierce minnows had attacked me and hung on like leeches. When a boy, I was—once or twice—a bait-fisher, but I never carried worms in box or bag. I found them under big stones, or in the fields, wherever I had the luck. I never tie nor otherwise fasten the joints of my rod; they often slip out of the sockets and splash into the water. Mr.

Hardy, however, has invented a joint-fastening which never slips. On the other hand, by letting the joint rust, you may find it difficult to take down your rod. When I see a trout rising, I always cast so as to get hung up, and I frighten him as I disengage my hook. I invariably fall in and get half-drowned when I wade, there being an insufficiency of nails in the soles of my brogues. My waders let in water, too, and when I go out to fish I usually leave either my reel, or my flies, or my rod, at home. Perhaps no other man's average of lost flies in proportion to taken trout was ever so great as mine. I lose plenty, by striking furiously, after a series of short rises, and breaking the gut, with which the fish swims away. As to dressing a fly, one would sooner think of dressing a dinner. The result of the fly-dressing would resemble a small blacking-brush, perhaps, but nothing entomological.

Then why, a persevering reader may ask, do I fish? Well, it is stronger than myself, the love of fishing; perhaps it is an inherited instinct, without the inherited power. I may have had a fishing ancestor who bequeathed to me the passion without the art. My vocation is fixed, and I have fished to little purpose all my days. Not for salmon, an almost fabulous and yet a stupid fish, which must be moved with a rod like a weaver's beam. The trout is more delicate and dainty—not the sea-trout, which any man, woman, or child can capture, but the yellow trout in clear water.

A few rises are almost all I ask for: to catch more than half a dozen fish does not fall to my lot twice a year. Of course, in a Sutherland loch one man is as good as another, the expert no better than the duffer. The fish will take, or they won't. If they won't, nobody can catch them; if they will, nobody can miss them. It is as simple as trolling a minnow from a boat in Loch Leven, probably the lowest possible form of angling. My ambition is as great as my skill is feeble; to capture big trout with the dry fly in the Test, that would content me, and nothing under that. But I can't see the natural fly on the water; I cannot see my own fly,

> Let it sink or let it swim.

I often don't see the trout rise to me, if he is such a fool as to rise; and I can't strike in time when I do see him. Besides, I am unteachable to tie any of the orthodox knots in the gut; it takes me half an hour to get the gut through one of these newfangled iron eyes, and, when it is through, I knot it any way. The "jam" knot is a name to me, and no more. That, perhaps, is why the hooks crack off so merrily. Then, if I do spot a rising trout, and if he does not spot me as I crawl like the serpent towards him, my fly always fixes in a nettle, a haycock, a rose-bush, or whatnot, behind me. I undo it, or break it, and put up another, make a cast, and, "plop," all the line falls in with a splash that would frighten a crocodile. The fish's big black fin goes cutting the stream above, and there is a *sauve qui peut* of trout in all directions.

I once did manage to make a cast correctly: the fly went over the fish's nose; he rose; I hooked him, and he was a great silly brute of a grayling. The grayling is the deadest-hearted and the foolishest-headed fish that swims. I would as lief catch a perch or an eel as a grayling. This is the worst of it—this ambition of the duffer's, this desire for perfection, as if the golfing imbecile should match himself against Mr. Horace Hutchinson, or as the sow of the Greek proverb challenged Athene to sing. I know it all, I deplore it, I regret the evils of ambition; but *c'est plus fort que moi*. If there is a trout rising well under the pendant boughs that trail in the water, if there is a brake of briars behind me, a strong wind down stream, for that trout, in that impregnable situation, I am impelled to fish. If I raise him I strike, miss him, catch up in his tree, swish the cast off into the briars, break my top, break my heart, but—that is the humour of it. The passion, or instinct, being in all senses blind, must no doubt be hereditary. It is full of sorrow and bitterness and hope deferred, and entails the mockery of friends, especially of the fair. But I would as soon lay down a love of books as a love of fishing.

Success with pen or rod may be beyond one,

but there is the pleasure of the pursuit, the rapture of endeavour, the delight of an impossible chase, the joys of nature—sky, trees, brooks, and birds. Happiness in these things is the legacy to us of the barbarian. Man in the future will enjoy bricks, asphalte, fog, machinery, "society," even picture galleries, as many men and most women do already. We are fortunate who inherit the older, not "the new spirit"—we who, skilled or unskilled, follow in the steps of our father, Izaak, by streams less clear, indeed, and in meadows less fragrant, than his. Still, they are meadows and streams, not wholly dispeopled yet of birds and trout; nor can any defect of art, nor certainty of laborious disappointment, keep us from the waterside when April comes.

Next to being an expert, it is well to be a contented duffer: a man who would fish if he could, and who will pleasure himself by flicking off his flies, and dreaming of impossible trout, and smoking among the sedges Hope's enchanted cigarettes. Next time we shall be more skilled, more fortunate. Next time! "To-morrow, and to-morrow, and to-morrow." Grey hairs come, and stiff limbs, and shortened sight; but the spring is green and hope is fresh for all the changes in the world and in ourselves. We can tell a hawk from a hand-saw, a March Brown from a Blue Dun; and if our success be as poor as ever, our fancy can dream as well as ever of better things and more fortunate chances. For fishing is like life; and in the art of living, too, there are duffers, though they seldom give us their confessions. Yet even they are kept alive, like the incompetent angler, by this undying hope: they will be more careful, more skilful, more lucky next time. The gleaming untravelled future, the bright untried waters, allure us from day to day, from pool to pool, till, like the veteran on Coquet side, we "try a farewell throw," or, like Stoddart, look our last on Tweed.

A Border Boyhood

~

A fisher, says our father Izaak, is like a poet: he "must be born so." The majority of dwellers on the Border are born to be fishers, thanks to the endless number of rivers and burns in the region between the Tweed and the Coquet—a realm where almost all trout-fishing is open, and where, since population and love of the sport have increased, there is now but little water that merits the trouble of putting up a rod.

Like the rest of us in that country, I was born an angler, though under an evil star, for, indeed, my labours have not been blessed, and are devoted to fishing rather than to the catching of fish. Remembrance can scarcely recover, "nor time bring back to time," the days when I was not busy at the waterside; yet the feat is not quite beyond the power of Mnemosyne. My first recollection of the sport must date from about the age of four. I recall, in a dim brightness, driving along a road that ran between banks of bracken and mica-veined rocks, and the sunlight on a shining bend of a highland stream, and my father, standing in the shallow water, showing me a huge yellow fish, that gave its last fling or two on the grassy bank. The fish seemed as terrible and dangerous to me as to Tobit, in the Apocrypha, did that ferocious half-pounder which he carries on a string in the early Italian pictures. How oddly Botticelli and his brethren misconceived the man-devouring fish, which must have been a crocodile strayed from the Nile into the waters of the Euphrates! A half-pounder! To have been terrified by a trout seems a bad beginning; and, thereafter, the mist gather's over the past, only to lift again when I see myself, with a crowd of other little children, sent to fish, with crooked pins, for minnows, or "baggies" as we called them, in the Ettrick. If our parents hoped that we would bring home minnows for bait, they were disappointed. The party was under the command of a nursery governess, and probably she was no descendant of the mother of us all, Dame Juliana Berners. We did not catch any minnows, and I remember sitting to watch a bigger boy, who was angling in a shoal of them when a parr came into the shoal, and we had bright visions of alluring that monarch of the deep. But the parr disdained our baits, and for months I dreamed of what it would have been to capture him, and often thought of him in church. In a moment of profane confidence my younger brother once asked me: "What do *you* do in sermon time? I," said he in a whisper—"mind you don't tell—*I* tell stories to myself about catching trout." To which I added similar confession, for even so I drove the sermon by, and I have not "told"—till now.

By this time we must have been introduced to trout. Who forgets his first trout? Mine, thanks to that unlucky star, was a double deception, or rather there were two kinds of deception. A village carpenter very kindly made rods for us. They were of unpainted wood, these first rods; they were in two pieces, with a real brass joint, and there was a ring at the end of the top joint, to which the line was knotted. We were still in the age of Walton, who clearly knew nothing, except by hearsay, of a reel; he abandons the attempt to describe that machine as used by the salmon-fishers. He thinks it must be seen to be understood. With these innocent weapons, and with the gardener to bait our hooks, we were taken to the Yarrow, far up the stream, near Ladhope. How well one remembers deserting the gardener, and already appreciating the joys of having no gillie nor attendant, of being "alone with ourselves and the goddess of fishing"! I cast away as well as I could, and presently jerked a trout, a tiny one, high up in the air out of the water. But he fell off the hook again, he dropped in with a little splash, and I rushed up to consult my tutor on his unsportsmanlike behaviour, and the disappointing, nay, heart-breaking, occurrence. Was the trout not morally caught, was there no way of getting him to see this and behave accordingly? The gardener feared there was none. Meanwhile he sat on the bank and angled in a pool.

"Try my rod," he said, and, as soon as I had taken hold of it, "pull up," he cried, "pull up." I did "pull up," and hauled my first troutling on shore. But in my inmost heart I feared that he was not my trout at all, that the gardener had hooked him before he handed the rod to me. Then we met my younger brother coming to us with quite a great fish, half a pound perhaps, which he had caught in a burn. Then, for the first time, my soul knew the fierce passion of jealousy, the envy of the angler. Almost for the last time, too; for, I know not why it is, and it proves me no true fisherman, I am not discontented by the successes of others. If one cannot catch fish oneself, surely the next best thing is to see other people catch them.

My own progress was now checked for long by a constitutional and insuperable aversion to angling with worm. If the gardener, or a pretty girl-cousin of the mature age of fourteen, would put the worm on, I did not "much mind" fishing with it. Dost thou remember, fair lady of the ringlets? Still, I never liked bait-fishing, and these mine allies were not always at hand. We used, indeed, to have great days with perch at Faldonside, on the land which Sir Walter Scott was always so anxious to buy from Mr. Nichol Milne. Almost the last entry in his diary, at Naples, breathes this unutterable hope. He had deluded himself into believing that his debts were paid, and that he could soon "speak a word to young Nichol

Milne." The word, of course, was never spoken, and the unsupplanted laird used to let us fish for his perch to our hearts' desire. Never was there such slaughter. The corks which we used as floats were perpetually tipping, bobbing, and disappearing, and then the red-finned perch would fly out on to dry land. Here I once saw two corks go down, two anglers haul up, and one perch, attached to both hooks, descend on the grassy bank. My brother and I filled two baskets once, and strung dozens of other perch on a stick.

But this was not legitimate business. Not till we came to fly-fishing were we really entered at the sport, and this initiation took place, as it chanced, beside the very stream where I was first shown a trout. It is a charming piece of water, amber-coloured and clear, flowing from the Morvern hills under the limes of an ancient avenue—trees that have long survived the house to which, of old, the road must have led. Our gillie put on for us big bright sea-trout flies—nobody fishes there for yellow trout; but, in our inexperience, small "brownies" were all we caught. Probably we were only taken to streams and shallows where we could not interfere with mature sportsmen. At all events, it was demonstrated to us that we could actually catch fish with fly, and since then I have scarcely touched a worm, except as a boy, in burns. In these early days we had no notion of playing a trout. If there was a bite, we put our strength into an answering tug, and, if nothing gave way, the trout flew over our heads, perhaps up into a tree, perhaps over into a branch of the stream behind us. Quite a large trout will yield to this artless method, if the rod be sturdy—none of your glued-up cane-affairs. I remember hooking a trout which, not answering to the first haul, ran right across the stream and made for a hole in the opposite bank. But the second lift proved successful and he landed on my side of the water. He had a great minnow in his throat, and must have been a particularly greedy animal. Of course, on this system there were many breakages, and the method was abandoned as we lived into our teens, and began to wade and to understand something about fly-fishing.

It was worth while to be a boy then in the south of Scotland, and to fish the waters haunted by old legends, musical with old songs, and renowned in the sporting essays of Christopher North and Stoddart. Even then, thirty long years ago, the old stagers used to tell us that "the waiter was owr sair fished," and they grumbled about the system of draining the land, which makes a river a roaring torrent in floods, and a bed of grey stones with a few clear pools and shallows, during the rest of the year. In times before the hills were drained, before the manufacturing towns were so populous, before pollution, netting, dynamiting, poisoning, sniggling, and the enormous increase of fair and unfair fishing, the border must have been the angler's paradise. Still, it was not bad when we were boys. We had Ettrick within a mile of us, and a finer natural trout-stream there is not in Scotland, though now the water only holds a sadly persecuted remnant. There was one long pool behind Lindean, flowing beneath a high wooded bank, where the trout literally seemed never to cease rising at the flies that dropped from the pendant boughs. Unluckily the water flowed out of the pool in a thin broad stream, directly it right angles to the pool itself. Thus the angler had, so to speak, the whole of lower Ettrick at his back when he waded: it was a long way up stream to the bank, and, as we never used landing-nets then, we naturally lost a great many trout in trying to unhook them in mid water. They only averaged as a rule from three to two to the pound, but they were strong and lively. In this pool there was a large tawny, table-shaped stone, over which the current broke. Out of the eddy behind this stone, one of my brothers one day caught three trout weighing over seven pounds, a feat which nowadays sounds quite incredible. As soon as the desirable eddy was empty, another trout, a trifle smaller than the former, seems to have occupied it. The next mile and a half, from Lindean to the junction with Tweed, was remarkable for excellent sport. In the last pool of Ettrick, the water flowed by a steep bank, and, if you cast almost on to the further side, you were perfectly safe to get fish, even when the river was very low. The flies used, three on a cast, were small and dusky, hare's ear and woodcock wing, black palmers, or, as Stoddart sings,

> Wee dour looking huiks are the thing,
> Mouse body and laverock wing.

Next to Ettrick came Tweed: the former river joins the latter at the bend of a long stretch of water, half stream, half pool, in which angling was always good. In late September there were sea-trout, which, for some reason, rose to the fly much more freely than sea-trout do now in the upper Tweed. I particularly remember hooking one just under the railway bridge. He was a two-pounder, and practised the usual sea-trout tactics of springing into the air like a rocket. There was a knot on my line, of course, and I was obliged to hold him hard. When he had been dragged up on the shingle, the line parted, broken in twain at the knot; but it had lasted just long enough, during three exciting minutes. This accident of a knot on the line has only once befallen me since, with the strongest loch-trout I ever encountered. It was on Branxholme Loch, where the trout run to a great size, but usually refuse the fly. I was alone in a boat on a windy day; the trout soon ran out the line to the knot, and then there was nothing for it but to lower the top almost to the water's edge, and hold on in hope. Presently the boat drifted ashore, and I landed him—better luck than I deserved. People who only know the trout of the Test and other chalk streams, cannot imagine how much stronger are the fish of the swift Scottish streams and dark Scottish lochs. They're worse fed, but they are infinitely more powerful and active; it is all the difference between an alderman and a clansman.

Tweed, at this time, was full of trout, but even then they were not easy to catch. One difficulty lay in the nature of the wading. There is a pool near Ashiesteil and Gleddis Weil which illustrated this. Here Scott and Hogg were once upset from a boat while "burning the water"—spearing salmon by torchlight. Herein, too, as Scott mentions in his Diary, he once caught two trout at one cast. The pool is long, is paved with small gravel, and allures you to wade on and on. But the water gradually deepens as you go forward, and the pool ends in a deep pot under each bank. Then to recover your ground becomes by no means easy, especially if the water is heavy. You get half-drowned, or drowned altogether, before you discover your danger. Many of the pools have this peculiarity, and in many, one step made rashly lets you into a very uncomfortable and perilous place. Therefore expeditions to Tweedside were apt to end in a ducking. It was often hard to reach the water where trout were rising, and the rise was always capricious. There might not be a stir on the water for hours, and suddenly it would be all boiling with heads and tails for twenty minutes, after which nothing was to be done. To miss "the take" was to waste the day, at least in fly-fishing. From a high wooded bank I have seen the trout feeding, and they have almost ceased to feed before I reached the waterside. Still worse was it to be allured into water over the tops of your waders, early in the day, and then to find that the rise was over, and there was nothing for it but a weary walk home, the basket laden only with damp boots. Still, the trout were undeniably *there*, and that was a great encouragement. They are there still, but infinitely more cunning than of old. Then, if they were feeding, they took the artificial fly freely; now it must be exactly of the right size and shade or they will have none of it. They come provokingly short, too; just plucking at the hook, and running out a foot of line or so, then taking their departure. For some reason the Tweed is more difficult to fish with the dry fly than—the Test, for example. The water is swifter and very dark, it drowns the fly soon, and on the surface the fly is less easily distinguished than at Whitchurch, in the pellucid streams. The Leader a tributary, may be fished with dry fly; on the Tweed one can hardly manage it. There is a plan by which rising trout may be taken—namely, by baiting with a small red worm and casting as in fly-fishing. But that is so hard on the worm! Probably he who can catch trout with fly on the Tweed between Melrose and Holy Lee can catch them anywhere. On a good day in April great baskets are still made in preserved parts of the Tweed, but, if they are made in open water, it must be, I fancy, with worm, or with the "screw," the lava of the May-fly. The screw is a hideous and venomous-looking animal, which is fixed on a particular kind of tackle, and cast up stream with a short line. The heaviest trout are fond of it, but it can only be used at a season when either school or Oxford keeps one far from what old Franck, Walton's contemporary, a Cromwellian trooper, calls "the glittering and resolute streams of Tweed."

Difficult as it is, that river is so beautiful and alluring that it scarcely needs the attractions of sport. The step banks, beautifully wooded, and in spring one mass of primroses, are crowned here and there with ruined Border towers—like Elibank, the houses of Muckle Mou'ed Meg; or with fair baronial houses like Fernilea. Meg made a bad exchange when she left Elibank with the salmon pool at its foot for bleak Harden, frowning over the narrow "den" where Harden kept the plundered cattle. There is no fishing in the tiny Harden burn, that joins the brawling Borthwick Water.

The burns of the Lowlands are now almost barren of trout. The spawning fish, flabby and useless, are killed in winter. All through the rest of the year, in the remotest places, tourists are hard at them with worm. In a small burn a skilled wormer may almost depopulate the pools, and, on the Border, all is fish that comes to the hook; men keep the very fingerlings, on the pretext that they are "so sweet" in the frying-pan. The crowd of anglers in glens which seem not easily accessible is provoking enough. Into the Meggat, a stream which feeds St. Mary's Loch, there flows the Glengaber, or Glencaber burn: the burn of the pine-tree stump. The water runs in deep pools and streams over a blue slatey rock, which contains gold under the sand, in the worn holes and crevices. My friend, Mr. McAllister, the schoolmaster at St. Mary's, tells me that one day, when fish were not rising, he scooped out the gravel of one of these holes with his knife, and found a tiny nugget, after which the gold-hunting fever came on him for a while. But little is got nowadays, though in some earlier period the burn has been diverted from its bed, and the people used solemnly to wash the sand, as in California or Australia. Well, whether in consequence of the gold, as the alchemical philosophers would have held, or not, the trout of the Glengaber burn were good. They were far shorter, thicker and stronger than those of the many neighbouring brooks. I have fished up the burn with fly, when it was very low, hiding carefully behind the boulders, and have been surprised at the size and gameness of the fish. As soon as the fly had touched the brown water, it was sucked down, and there was quite a fierce little fight before the fish came to hand.

"This, all this, was in the olden time, long ago."

The Glengaber burn is about twenty miles from any railway station, but, on the last occasion when I visited it, three louts were worming their way up it, within twenty yards of each other, each lout, with his huge rod, showing himself wholly to any trout that might be left in the water. Thirty years ago the burns that feed St. Mary's Loch were almost unfished, and rare sport we had in them, as boys, staying at Tibbie Sheil's famous cottage, and sleeping in her box-beds, where so often the Ettrick Shepherd and Christopher North have lain, after copious toddy. "'Tis gone, 'tis gone:" not in our time will any man, like the Ettrick Shepherd, need a cart to carry the trout he has slain in Meggat Water. That stream, flowing through a valley furnished with a grass-grown track for a road, flows, as I said, into St. Mary's Loch. There are two or three large pools at the foot of the loch, in which, as a small boy hardly promoted to fly, I have seen many monsters rising greedily. Men got into the way of fishing these pools after a flood with minnow, and thereby made huge baskets, the big fish running up to feed, out of the loch. But, when last I rowed past Meggat foot, the delta of that historic stream was simply crowded with anglers, stepping in in front of each other. I asked if this mob was a political "demonstration," but they stuck to business, as if they had been on the Regent's

Canal. And this, remember, was twenty miles from any town! Yet there is a burn on the Border still undiscovered, still full of greedy trout. I shall give the angler such a hint of its whereabouts as Tiresias, in Hades, gave to Odysseus concerning the end of his second wanderings.

When, O stranger, thou hast reached a burn where the shepherd asks thee for the newspaper wrapped round thy sandwiches, that he may read the news, then erect an altar to Priapus, god of fishermen, and begin to angle boldly.

Probably the troops who fish our Border-burns still manage to toss out some dozens of tiny fishes, some six or eight to the pound. Are not these triumphs chronicled in the "Scotsman?" But they cannot imagine what angling was in the dead years, nor what great trout dwelt below the linns of the Crosscleugh burn, beneath the red clusters of the rowan trees, or in the waters of the "Little Yarrow" above the Loch of the Lowes. As to the lochs themselves, now that anyone may put a boat on them, now that there is perpetual trolling, as well as fly-fishing, so that every fish knows the lures, the fun is mainly over. In April, no doubt, something may still be done, and in the silver twilights of June, when as you drift on the still surface you hear the constant sweet plash of the rising trout, a few, and these good, may be taken. But the water wants re-stocking, and the burns in winter need watching, in the interests of spawning fish. It is nobody's interest, that I know of, to take trouble and incur expense; and free fishing, by the constitution of the universe, must end in bad fishing or in none at all. The best we can say for it is that vast numbers of persons may, by the still waters of these meres, enjoy the pleasures of hope. Even solitude is no longer to be found in the scene which Scott, in "Marmion," chooses as of all places the most solitary.

> Here, have I thought, 'twere sweet to dwell,
> And rear again the chaplain's cell.

But no longer does

> "Your horse's hoof tread sound too rude,
> So stilly is the solitude."

Stilly! with the horns and songs from omnibusses that carry tourists, and with yells from nymphs and swains disporting themselves in the boats. Yarrow is only the old Yarrow in winter. Ages and revolutions must pass before the ancient peace returns; and only if the golden age is born again, and if we revive in it, shall we find St. Mary's what St. Mary's was lang syne—

> Ah, Buddha, if thy tale be true,
>   Of still returning life,
> A monk may I be born anew,
>   In valleys free from strife,—

A monk where Meggat winds and laves
The lone St. Mary's of the Waves.

Yarrow, which flows out of St. Mary's Loch was
never a great favourite of mine, as far as fishing goes. It had,
and probably deserved, a great reputation, and some good
trout are still taken in the upper waters, and there must be
monsters in the deep black pools, the "dowie dens" above
Bowhill. But I never had any luck there. The choicest
stream of all was then, probably, the Aill, described by Sir
Walter in "William of Deloraine's Midnight Ride"—

> Where Aill, from mountains freed,
> Down from the lakes did raving come;
> Each wave was crested with tawny foam,
> Like the mane of a chestnut steed.

As not uncommonly happens, Scott uses rather
large language here. The steepy, grassy hillsides,
the great green tablelands in a recess of which the
Aill is born, can hardly be called "mountains." The
"lakes," too, through which it passes, are much more
like tarns, or rather, considering the flatness of their
banks, like well-meaning ponds. But the Aill, near
Sinton and Ashkirk, was a delightful trout-stream,
between its willow-fringed banks, a brook about the
size of the Lambourne. Nowhere on the Border were
trout more numerous, better fed, and more easily
beguiled. A week on Test would I gladly give for one
day of boyhood beside the Aill, where the casting was

not scientific, but where the fish rose gamely at almost any fly. Nobody seemed to go there then, and, I fancy, nobody need go there now. The nets and other dismal devices of the poachers from the towns have ruined that pleasant brook, where one has passed so many a happy hour, walking the long way home wet and weary, but well content. Into Aill flows a burn, the Headshaw burn, where there used to be good fish, because it runs out of Headshaw Loch, a weed-fringed lonely tarn on the bleak level of the tableland. Bleak as it may seem, Headshaw Loch has the great charm of absolute solitude: there are no tourists nor anglers here, and the life of the birds is especially free and charming. The trout, too, are large, pink of flesh, and game of character; but the world of mankind need not rush thither. They are not to be captured by the wiles of men, or so rarely that the most enthusiastic anglers have given them up. They are as safe in their tarn as those enchanted fish of the "Arabian Nights." Perhaps a silver sedge in a warm twilight may somewhat avail, but the adventure is rarely achieved.

These are the waters with which our boyhood was mainly engaged; it is a pleasure to name and number them. Memory, that has lost so much and would gladly lose so much more, brings vividly back the golden summer evenings by Tweedside, when the trout began to plash in the stillness—brings back the long, lounging, solitary days beneath the woods of Ashiesteil—days so lonely that they sometimes, in the end, begat a superstitious eeriness. One seemed forsaken in an enchanted world; one might see the two white fairy deer flit by, bringing to us, as to Thomas Rhymer, the tidings that we must back to Fairyland. Other waters we knew well, and loved: the little salmon-stream in the west that doubles through the loch, and runs a mile or twain beneath its alders, past its old Celtic battle-field, beneath the ruined shell of its feudal tower, to the sea. Many a happy day we had there, on loch or stream, with the big sea-trout which have somehow changed their tastes, and to-day take quite different flies from the green body and the red body that led them to the landing-net long ago. Dear are the twin Alines, but dearer is Tweed, and Ettrick, where our ancestor was drowned in a flood, and his white horse was found, next day, feeding near his dead body, on a little grassy island. There is a great pleasure in trying new methods, in labouring after the delicate art of the dry fly-fisher in the clear Hampshire streams, where the glassy tide flows over the waving tresses of crow's-foot below the poplar shade. But nothing can be so good as what is old, and, as far as angling goes, is practically ruined, the alternate pool and stream of the Border waters, where

> The triple pride
> Of Eildon looks over Strathclyde,

and the salmon cast murmurs hard by the Wizard's grave. They are all gone now, the old allies and tutors in the angler's art—the kind gardener who baited our hooks; the good Scotch judge who gave us our first collection of flies; the friend who took us with him on his salmon-fishing expedition, and made men of us with real rods, and "pirns" of ancient make. The companions of those times are scattered, and live under strange stars and in converse seasons, by troutless waters. It is no longer the height of pleasure to be half-drowned in Tweed, or lost on the hills with no luncheon in the basket. But, except for scarcity of fish, the scene is very little altered, and one is a boy again, in heart, beneath the elms of Yair, or by the Gullets at Ashiesteil. However bad the sport, it keeps you young, or makes you young again, and you need not follow Ponce de Léon to the western wilderness, when, in any river you knew of yore, you can find the Fountain of Youth.

LOCH AWE

~

THE BOATMAN'S YARNS

Good trout-fishing in Scotland, south of the Pentland Firth, is almost impossible to procure. There are better fish, and more of them, in the Wandle, within twenty minutes of Victoria Station, than in any equal stretch of any Scotch river with which I am acquainted. But the pleasure of angling, luckily, does not consist merely of the catching of fish. The Wandle is rather too suburban for some tastes, which prefer smaller trout, better air, and wilder scenery. To such spirits, Loch Awe may, with certain distinct cautions, be recommended. There is more chance for anglers, now, in Scotch lochs than in most Scotch rivers. The lochs cannot so easily be netted, lined, polluted, and otherwise made empty and ugly, like the Border streams. They are farther off from towns and tourists, though distance is scarcely a complete protection. The best lochs for yellow trout are decidedly those of Sutherland. There are no railways, and there are two hundred lochs and more in the Parish of Assynt. There, in June, the angler who is a good pedestrian may actually enjoy solitude, sometimes. There is a loch near Strathnaver, and far from human habitations, where a friend of my own recently caught sixty-five trout weighing about thirty-eight pounds. They are numerous and plucky, but not large, though a casual big loch-trout may be taken by trolling. But it is truly a far way to this anonymous lake and all round the regular fishing inns, like Inchnadampf and Forsinard there is usually quite a little crowd of anglers. The sport is advertised in the newspapers; more and more of our eager fellow-creatures are attracted, more and more the shooting tenants are preserving waters that used to be open. The distance to Sutherland makes that county almost beyond the range of a brief holiday. Loch Leven is nearer, and at Loch Leven the scenery is better than its reputation, while the trout are excellent, though shy. But Loch Leven is too much cockneyfied by angling competitions; moreover, its pleasures are expensive. Loch Awe remains, a loch at once large, lovely, not too distant, and not destitute of sport.

The reader of Mr. Colquhoun's delightful old book, "The Moor and the Loch," must not expect Loch Awe to be what it once was. The railway, which has made the north side of the lake so ugly, has brought the district within easy reach of Glasgow and of Edinburgh. Villas are built on many a beautiful height; here couples come for their honeymoon, here whole argosies of boats are anchored off the coasts, here do steam launches ply. The hotels are extremely comfortable, the boatmen are excellent boatmen, good fishers, and capital company. All this is pleasant, but all this attracts multitudes of anglers, and it is not in nature that sport should be what it once was. Of the famous *salmo ferox* I cannot speak from experience. The huge courageous fish is still at home in Loch Awe, but now he sees a hundred baits, natural and artificial, where he saw one in Mr. Colquhoun's time. The truly contemplative man may still sit in the stern of the boat, with two rods out, and possess his soul in patience, as if he were fishing for tarpon in Florida. I wish him luck, but the diversion is little to my mind. Except in playing the fish, if he comes, all the skill is in the boatmen, who know where to row, at what pace, and in what depth of water. As to the chances of salmon again, they are perhaps less rare, but they are not very frequent. The fish does not seem to take freely in the loch, and on his way from the Awe to the Orchy. As to the trout-fishing, it is very bad in the months when most men take their holidays, August and September. From the middle of April to the middle of June is apparently the best time. The loch is well provided with bays, of different merit, according to the feeding which they provide; some come earlier, some later into season. Doubtless the most beautiful part of the lake is around the islands, between the Loch Awe and the Port Sonachan hotels. The Green Island, with its strange Celtic burying-ground, where the daffodils bloom among the sepulchres with their rude carvings of battles and of armed men, has many trout around its shores. The favourite fishing-places, however, are between Port Sonachan and Ford. In the morning early, the steam-launch tows a fleet of boats down the loch, and they drift back again, fishing all the bays, and arriving at home in time for dinner. Too frequently the angler is vexed by finding a boat busy in his favourite bay. I am not sure that, when the trout are really taking, the water near Port Sonachan is not as good as any other. Much depends on the weather. In the hard north-east winds of April we can scarcely expect trout to feed very freely anywhere. These of Loch Awe are very peculiar fish. I take it that there are two species—one short, thick, golden, and beautiful; but these, at least in April, are decidedly scarce. The common sort is long, lanky, of a dark green hue, and the reverse of lovely. Most of them, however, are excellent at breakfast, pink in the flesh, and better flavoured, I think, than the famous trout of Loch Leven. They are also extremely game for their size; a half-pound trout fights like a pounder. From thirty to forty fish in a day's incessant angling is reckoned no bad basket. In genial May weather, probably the trout average two to the pound, and a pounder or two may be in the dish. But three to the pound is decidedly nearer the average, at least in April. The flies commonly used are larger than what are employed in Loch Leven. A teal wing and red body, a grouse hackle, and the prismatic Heckham Peckham are among the favourites; but it is said that flies no bigger than Tweed flies are occasionally successful. In my own brief experience I have found the trout "dour," occasionally they would rise freely for an hour at noon, or in the evening; but often one passed hours with scarcely a rising fish. This may have been due to the bitterness of the weather, or to my own lack of skill. Not that lochs generally require much artifice in the angler. To sink the flies deep, and move them with short jerks, appears, now and then, to be efficacious. There has been some controversy about Loch Awe trouting; this is as favourable a view of the sport as I can honestly give. It is not excellent, but, thanks to the great beauty of the scenery, the many points of view on so large and indented a lake, the charm of the wood and wild flowers, Loch Awe is well worth a visit from persons who do not pitch their hopes too high.

Loch Awe would have contented me less had I been less fortunate in my boatman. It is often said that tradition has died out in the Highlands; it is living yet.

After three days of north wind and failure, it occurred to me that my boatman might know the local folklore—the fairy tales and traditions. As a rule, tradition is a purely professional part of a guide's stock-in-trade, but the angler who had my barque in his charge proved to be a fresh fountain of legend. His own county is not Argyleshire, but Inverness, and we did not deal much in local myth. True, he told me why Loch Awe ceased—like the site of Sodom and Gomorrah—to be a cultivated valley and became a lake, where the trout are small and, externally, green.

"Loch Awe was once a fertile valley, and it belonged to an old dame. She was called Dame Cruachan, the same as the hill, and she lived high up on the hillside. Now there was a well on the hillside, and she was always to cover up the well with a big stone before the sun set. But one day she had been working in the valley and she was weary, and she sat down by the path on her way home and fell asleep. And the sun had gone down before she reached the well, and in the night the water broke out and filled all the plain, and what was land is now water." This, then, was the origin of Loch Awe. It is a little like the Australian account of the Deluge. That calamity was produced by a man's showing a woman the mystic turndun, a native sacred toy. Instantly water broke out of the earth and drowned everybody.

This is merely a local legend, such as boatmen are expected to know. As the green trout utterly declined to rise, I tried the boatman with the Irish story of why the Gruagach Gaire left off laughing, and all about the hare that came and defiled his table, as recited by Mr. Curtin in his "Irish Legends" (Sampson, Low, & Co.).

The boatman did not know this fable, but he did know of a red deer that came and spoke to a gentleman. This was a story from the Macpherson country. I give it first in the boatman's words, and then we shall discuss the history of the legend as known to Sir Walter Scott and James Hogg, the Ettrick Shepherd.

THE YARN OF THE BLACK OFFICER

"It was about 'the last Christmas of the hundred'—the end of last century. They wanted men for the Black Watch (42nd Highlanders), and the Black Officer, as they called him, was sent to his own country to enlist them. Some he got willingly, and others by force. He promised he would only take them to London, where the King wanted to review them, and then let them go home. So they came, though they little liked it, and he was marching them south. Now at night they reached a place where nobody would have halted them except the Black Officer, for it was a great place for ghosts. And they would have run away if they had dared, but they were afraid of him. So some tried to sleep in threes and fours, and some were afraid to sleep, and they sat up round the fire. But the Black Officer, he went some way from the rest, and lay down beneath a tree.

"Now as the night wore on, and whiles it would

41

be dark and whiles the moon shone, a man came—they did not know from where—a big red man, and drew up to the fire, and was talking with them. And he asked where the Black Officer was, and they showed him. Now there was one man, Shamus Mackenzie they called him, and he was very curious, and he must be seeing what they did. So he followed the man, and saw him stoop and speak to the officer, but he did not waken; then this individual took the Black Officer by the breast and shook him violently. Then Shamus knew who the stranger was, for no man alive durst have done as much to the Black Officer. And there was the Black Officer kneeling to him!

"Well, what they said, Shamus could not hear, and presently they walked away, and the Black Officer came back alone.

"He took them to England, but never to London, and they never saw the King. He took them to Portsmouth, and they were embarked for India, where we were fighting the French. There was a town we couldn't get into" (Seringapatam?), "and the Black Officer volunteered to make a tunnel under the walls. Now they worked three days, and whether it was the French heard them and let them dig on, or not, any way, on the third day the French broke in on them. They kept sending men into the tunnel, and more men, and still they wondered who was fighting within, and how we could have so large a party in the tunnel; so at last they brought torches, and there was no man alive on our side but the Black Officer, and he had a wall of corpses built up in front of him, and was fighting across it. He had more light to see by than the French had, for it was dark behind him, and there would be some light on their side. So at last they brought some combustibles and blew it all up. Three days after that we took the town. Some of our soldiers were sent to dig out the tunnel, and with them was Shamus Mackenzie."

"And they never found the Black Officer," I said, thinking of young Campbell in Sekukoeni's fighting koppie.

"Oh, yes," said the boatman, "Shamus found the body of the Black Officer, all black with smoke, and he laid him down on a green knoll, and was standing over the dead man, and was thinking of how many places they had been in together, and of his own country, and how he wished he was there again. Then the dead man's face moved.

"Shamus turned and ran for his life, and he was running till he met some officers, and he told them that the Black Officer's body had stirred. They thought he was lying, but they went off to the place, and one of them had the thought to take a flask of brandy in his pocket. When they came to the lifeless body it stirred again, and with one thing and another they brought him round.

"The Black Officer was not himself again for long, and they took him home to his own country, and he lay in bed in his house. And every day a red deer would come to the house, and go into his room and sit on a chair beside the bed, speaking to him like a man.

"Well, the Black Officer got better again, and went about among his friends; and once he was driving home from a dinner-party, and Shamus was with him. It was just the last night of the hundred. And on the road they met a man, and Shamus knew him—for it was him they had seen by the fire on the march, as I told you at the beginning. The Black Officer got down from his carriage and joined the man, and they walked a bit apart; but Shamus—he was so curious—whatever happened he must see them. And he came within hearing just as they were parting, and he heard the stranger say, 'This is the night.'

"'No,' said the Black Officer, 'this night next year.'

"So he came back, and they drove home. A year went by, and the Black Officer was seeking through the country for the twelve best men he could find to accompany him to some deer-hunt or the like. And he asked Shamus, but he pretended he was ill—Oh, he was very unwell!—and he could not go, but stayed in bed at home. So the Black Officer chose another man, and he and the twelve set out—the thirteen of them.

But they were never seen again."

"Never seen again? Were they lost in the snow?"

"It did come on a heavy fall, sir."

"But their bodies were found?"

"No, sir—though they searched high and low; they are not found, indeed, till this day. It was thought the Black Officer had sold himself and twelve other men, sir."

"To the Devil?"

"It would be that."

For the narrator never mentions our ghostly foe, which produces a solemn effect.

This story was absolutely new to me, and much I wished that Mr. Louis Stevenson could have heard it. The blending of the far East with the Highlands reminds one of his "Master of Ballantrae," and what might he not make of that fairy red deer! My boatman, too, told me what Mr. Stevenson says the Highlanders will not tell—the name of the man who committed the murder of which Alan Breck was accused. But this secret I do not intend to divulge.

The story of the Black Officer then seemed absolutely unpublished. But when Sir Walter Scott's diary was given to the world in October, 1890, it turned out that he was not wholly ignorant of the legend. In 1828 he complains that he has been annoyed by a lady, because he had printed "in the 'Review'" a rawhead and bloody-bones story of her father, Major

Macpherson, who was lost in a snowstorm. This Major Macpherson was clearly the Black Officer. Mr. Douglas, the publisher of Scott's diary, discovered that the "Review" mentioned vaguely by Scott was the "Foreign Quarterly," No. I, July, 1827. In an essay on Hoffmann's novels, Sir Walter introduced the tale as told to him in a letter from a nobleman some time deceased, not more distinguished for his love of science than his attachment to literature in all its branches.

The tale is too long to be given completely. Briefly, a Captain M., on St. Valentine's day, 1799, had been deer-shooting (at an odd time of the year) in the hills west of D-. He did not return, a terrible snowstorm set in, and finally he and his friends were found dead in a bothy, which the tempest had literally destroyed. Large stones from the walls were found lying at distances of a hundred yards; the wooden uprights were twisted like broken sticks. The Captain was lying dead, without his clothes, on the bed; one man was discovered at a distance, another near the Captain. Then it was remembered that, at the same bothy a month before, a shepherd lad had inquired for the Captain, had walked with him for some time, and that, on the officer's return, "a mysterious anxiety hung about him." A fire had also been seen blazing on an opposite height, and when some of the gillies went to the spot, "there was no fire to be seen." On the day when the expedition had started, the Captain was warned of the ill weather, but he said "he *must* go." He was an unpopular man, and was accused of getting money by procuring recruits from the Highlands, often by cruel means. "Our informer told us nothing more; he neither told us his own opinion, nor that of the country, but left it to our own notions of the manner in which good and evil is rewarded in this life to suggest the author of the miserable event. He seemed impressed with superstitious awe on the subject, and said, 'There was na the like seen in a' Scotland.' The man is far advanced in years and is a schoolmaster in the neighbourhood of Rannoch."

Sir Walter says that "the feeling of superstitious awe annexed to the catastrophe could not have been improved by any circumstances of additional horror which a poet could have invented." But is there not something more moving still in the boatman's version: "they were never seen again . . . they were not found indeed till this day"?

The folklorist, of course, is eager to know whether the boatman's much more complete and connected narrative is a popular mythical development in the years between 1820 and 1890, or whether the schoolmaster of Rannoch did not tell all he knew. It is unlikely, I think, that the siege of Seringapatam would have been remembered so long in connection with the Black Officer if it had not formed part of his original legend. Meanwhile the earliest printed notice of the event with which I am acquainted, a notice only ten years later than the date of the Major's death in 1799, is given by Hogg in "The Spy," 1810-11, pp. 101-3. I offer an abridgment of the narrative.

"About the end of last century Major Macpherson and a party of friends went out to hunt on the Grampians between Athole and Badenoch. They were highly successful, and in the afternoon they went into a little bothy, and, having meat and drink, they abandoned themselves to jollity.

"During their merry-making a young man entered whose appearance particularly struck and somewhat shocked Macpherson; the stranger beckoned to the Major, and he followed him instantly out of the bothy.

"When they parted, after apparently having had some earnest conversation, the stranger was out of sight long before the Major was half-way back, though only twenty yards away.

"The Major showed on his return such evident marks of trepidation that the mirth was marred and no one cared to ask him questions.

"This was early in the week, and on Friday the Major persuaded his friends to make a second expedition to the mountains, from which they never returned.

"On a search being made their dead bodies

were found in the bothy, some considerably mangled, but some were not marked by any wound.

"It was visible that this had not been effected by human agency: the bothy was torn from its foundations and scarcely a vestige left of it, and one huge stone, which twelve men could not have raised, was tossed to a considerable distance.

"On this event Scott's beautiful ballad of 'Glenfinlas' is said to have been founded."

As will be seen presently, Hogg was wrong about 'Glenfinlas'; the boatman was acquainted with a traditional version of that wild legend. I found another at Rannoch.

The Highland fairies are very vampirish. The Loch Awe boatman lives at a spot haunted by a shadowy maiden. Her last appearance was about thirty years ago. Two young men were thrashing corn one morning, when the joint of the flail broke. The owner went to Larichban and entered an outhouse to look for a piece of sheepskin wherewith to mend the flail. He was long absent, and his companion went after him. He found him struggling in the arms of a ghostly maid, who had nearly murdered him, but departed on the arrival of his friend. It is not easy to make out what these ghoulish women are—not fairies exactly, nor witches, nor vampires. For example, three shepherds at a lonely sheiling were discoursing of their loves, and it was, "Oh, how happy I should be if Katie were here, or Maggie, or Bessie!" as the case might be. So they would say and so they would wish, and lo! one evening, the three girls came to the door of the hut. So they made them welcome; but one of the shepherds was playing the Jew's-harp, and he did not like the turn matters were taking.

The two others stole off into corners of the darkling hut with their lovers, but this prudent lad never took his lips off the Jew's-harp.

"Harping is good if no ill follows it," said the semblance of his sweetheart; but he never answered. He played and thrummed, and out of one dark corner trickled red blood into the fire-light, and out of another corner came a current of blood to meet it. Then he slowly rose, still harping, and backed his way to the door, and fled into the hills from these cruel airy shapes of false desire.

"And do the people actually believe all that?"

"Ay, do they!"

That is the boatman's version of Scott's theme in "Glenfinlas." Witches played a great part in his narratives.

In the boatman's country there is a plain, and on the plain is a knoll, about twice the height of a one-storeyed cottage, and pointed "like a sugar-loaf." The old people remember, or have heard, that this mound was not there when they were young. It swelled up suddenly out of the grave of a witch who was buried there.

The witch was a great enemy of a shepherd. Every morning she would put on the shape of a hare, and run before his dogs, and lead them away from the sheep. He knew it was right to shoot at her with a crooked sixpence, and he hit her on the hind leg, and the dogs were after her, and chased the hare into the old woman's cottage. The shepherd ran after them, and there he found them, tearing at the old woman; but the hare was twisted round their necks, and she was crying, "Tighten, hare, tighten!" and it was choking them. So he tore the hare off the dogs; and then the old woman begged him to save her from them, and she promised never to plague him again. "But if the old dog's teeth had been as sharp as the young one's, she would have been a dead woman."

When this witch died she knew she could never lie in safety in her grave; but there was a very safe churchyard in Aberdeenshire, a hundred and fifty miles away, and if she could get into that she would be at rest. And she rose out of her grave, and off she went, and the Devil after her, on a black horse; but, praise to the swiftness of her feet, she won the churchyard before him. Her first grave swelled up, oh, as high as that green hillock!

Witches are still in active practice. There was an old woman very miserly. She would alway be taking one of her neighbours' sheep from the hills, and they stood it for long; they did not like to meddle with her. At last it grew so bad that they brought her before the sheriff, and she got eighteen months in prison. When she came out she was very angry, and set about making an image of the woman whose sheep she had taken. When the image was made she burned it and put the ashes in a burn. And it is a very curious thing, but the woman she made it on fell into a decline, and took to her bed.

The witch and her family went to America. They kept a little inn, in a country place, and people who slept in it did not come out again. They were discovered, and the eldest son was hanged; he confessed that he had committed nineteen murders before he left Scotland.

"They were not a nice family."

"The father was a very respectable old man."

The boatman gave me the name of this wicked household, but it is perhaps better forgotten.

The extraordinary thing is that this appears to be the Highland introduction to, or part first of, a gloomy and sanguinary story of a murder hole—an inn of assassins in a lonely district of the United States, which Mr. Louis Stevenson heard in his travels there, and told to me some years ago. The details have escaped my memory, but, as Mr. Stevenson narrated them, they rivalled De Quincey's awful story of Williams's murders in the Ratcliffe Highway.

Life must still be haunted in Badenoch, as it was on Ida's hill, by forms of unearthly beauty, the goddess or the ghost yet wooing the shepherd; indeed, the boatman told me many stories of living superstition and terrors of the night; but why should I exhaust his wallet? To be sure, it seemed very full of tales; these offered here may be but the legends which came first to his hand. The boatman is not himself a believer in the fairy world, or not more than all sensible men ought to be. The supernatural is too pleasant a thing for us to discard in an earnest, scientific manner like Mr. Kipling's Aurelian McGubben. Perhaps I am more superstitious than the boatman, and the yarns I swopped with him about ghosts I have met would seem even more mendacious to possessors of pocket microscopes and of the modern spirit. But I would rather have one banshee story than fifteen pages of proof that "life, which began as a cell, with a c, is to end as a sell, with an s." It should be added that the boatman has given his consent to the printing of his yarns. On being offered a moiety of the profits, he observed that he had no objection to these, but that he entirely declined to be responsible for any share of the expenses. Would that all authors were as sagacious, for then the amateur novelist and the minor poet would vex us no more.

Perhaps I should note that I have not made the boatman say "whateffer," because he doesn't. The occasional use of the imperfect is almost his only Gaelic idiom. It is a great comfort and pleasure, when the trout do not rise, to meet a skilled and unaffected narrator of the old beliefs, old legends, as ancient as the hills that girdle and guard the loch, or as antique, at least, as man's dwelling among the mountains—the Yellow Hill, the Calf Hill, the Hill of the Stack. The beauty of the scene, the pleasant talk, the daffodils on the green isle among the Celtic graves, compensate for a certain "dourness" among the fishes of Loch Awe. On the occasions when they are not dour they rise very pleasant and free, but, in these brief moments, it is not of legends and folklore that you are thinking, but of the landing-net. The boatman, by the way, was either not well acquainted with *Märchen*—Celtic nursery-tales such as Campbell of Islay collected, or was not much interested in them, or, perhaps, had the shyness about narrating this particular sort of old wives' fables which is so common. People who do know them seldom tell them in Sassenach.

LOCH-FISHING

~

LITTLE LOCH BEG

There is something mysterious in loch-fishing, in the tastes and habits of the fish which inhabit the innumerable lakes and tarns of Scotland. It is not always easy to account either for their presence or their absence, for their numbers or scarcity, their eagerness to take or their "dourness." For example, there is Loch Borlan, close to the well-known little inn of Alt-na-geal-gach in Sutherland. Unless that piece of water is greatly changed, it is simply full of fish of about a quarter of a pound, which will rise at almost any time to almost any fly. There is not much pleasure in catching such tiny and eager trout, but in the season complacent anglers capture and boast of their many dozens. On the other hand, a year or two ago, a beginner took a four-pound trout there with the fly. If such trout exist in Borlan, it is hard to explain the presence of the innumerable fry. One would expect the giants of the deep to keep down their population. Not far off is another small lake, Loch Awe, which has invisible advantages over Loch Borlan, yet there the trout are, or were, "fat and fair of flesh," like Tamlane in the ballad. Wherefore are the trout in Loch Tummell so big and strong, from one to five pounds, and so scarce, while those in Loch Awe are numerous and small? One occasionally sees examples of how quickly trout will increase in weight, and what curious habits they will adopt. In a county of south-western Scotland there is a large village, populated by a keenly devoted set of anglers, who miss no opportunity. Within a quarter of a mile of the village is a small tarn, very picturesquely situated among low hills, and provided with the very tiniest feeder and outflow. There is a sluice at the outflow, and, for some reason, the farmer used to let most of the water out, in the summer of every year. In winter the tarn is used by the curling club. It is not deep, has rather a marshy bottom, and many ducks, snipe, and wild-fowl generally dwell among the reeds and marish plants of its sides. Nobody ever dreamed of fishing here, but one day a rustic, "glowering" idly over the wall of the adjacent road, saw fish rising. He mentioned his discovery to an angler, who is said to have caught some large trout, but tradition varies about everything, except that the fish are very "dour." One evening in August, a warm, still evening, I happened to visit the tarn. As soon as the sun fell below the hills, it was literally alive with large trout rising. As far as one could estimate from the brief view of heads and shoulders, they were sometimes two or three pounds in weight. I got my rod, of course, as did a rural friend. Mine was a small cane rod, his a salmon-rod. I fished with one Test-fly; he with three large loch-flies. The fish were rising actually at our feet, but they seemed to move about very much, never, or seldom, rising twice exactly at the same place. The hypothesis was started that there were but few of them, and that they ran round and round, like a stage army, to give an appearance of multitude. But this appears improbable. What is certain was our utter inability ever to get a rise from the provoking creatures. The dry fly is difficult to use on a loch, as there is no stream to move it, and however gently you draw it it makes a "wake"—a trail behind it. Wet or dry, or "twixt wet and dry," like the convivial person in the song, we could none of us raise them. I did catch a small but beautifully proportioned and pink-fleshed trout with the alder, but everything else, silver sedge and all, everything from midge to May-fly, in the late twilight, was offered to them in vain. In windy or cloudy weather it was just as useless; indeed, I never saw them rise, except in a warm summer stillness, at and after sunset. Probably they would have taken a small red worm, pitched into the ripple of a rise; but we did not try that. After a few evenings, they seemed to give up rising altogether. I don't feel certain that they had not been netted: yet no trout seemed to be on sale in the village. Their presence in the water may perhaps be accounted for thus: they may have come into the loch from the river, by way of the tiny feeder; but the river-trout are both scarce and small. A new farmer had given up letting the water off, and probably there must have been very rich feeding, water-shrimps or snails, which might partly account for the refusal to rise at the artificial fly. Or they may have been ottered by the villagers, though that would rather have made them rise short than not rise at all.

There is another loch on an extremely remote hillside, eight miles from the smallest town, in a pastoral country. There are trout enough in the loch, and of excellent size and flavour, but you scarcely ever get them. They rise freely, but they always rise short. It is, I think, the most provoking loch I ever fished. You raise them; they come up freely, showing broad sides of a ruddy gold, like the handsomest Test trout, but they almost invariably miss the hook. You do not land one out of twenty. The reason is, apparently, that people from the nearest town use the otter in the summer evenings, when these trout rise best. In a Sutherland loch, Mr. Edward Moss tells us (in "A Season in Sutherland"), that he once found an elegant otter, a well-made engine of some unscrupulous tourist, lying in the bottom of the water on a sunny day. At Loch Skene, on the top of a hill, twenty miles from any town, otters are occasionally found by the keeper or the shepherds, concealed near the shore. The practice of ottering can give little pleasure to any but a depraved mind, and nothing educates trout so rapidly into "rising short"; why they are not to be had when they are rising most vehemently, "to themselves," is another mystery. A few rises are encouraging, but when the water is all splashing with rises, as a rule the angler is only tantalised. A windy day, a day with a large ripple, but without white waves breaking, is, as a rule, best for a loch. In some lochs the sea-trout prefer such a hurricane that a boat can hardly be kept on the water. I have known a strong north wind in autumn put down the sea-trout, whereas the salmon rose, with unusual eagerness, just in the shallows where the waves broke in foam on the shore. The best day I ever had with sea-trout was muggy and grey, and the fish were most eager when the water was still, except for a tremendously heavy shower of rain, "a singing shower," as George Chapman has it. On that day two rods caught thirty-nine sea-trout, weighing forty pounds. But it is difficult to say beforehand what day will do well, except that sunshine is bad, a north wind worse, and no wind at all usually means an empty basket. Even to this rule there are exceptions, and one of these is in the case of a tarn which I shall call, pleonastically, Little Loch Beg.

This is not the real name of the loch—quite enough people know its real name already. Nor does it seem necessary to mention the district where the loch lies hidden; suffice it to say that a land of more streams and scarcer trout you will hardly find. We had tried all the rivers and burns to no purpose, and the lochs are capricious and overfished. One loch we had not tried, Loch Beg. You walk, or drive, a few miles from any village, then you climb a few hundred yards of hill, and from the ridge you see, on one hand a great amphitheatre of green and purple mountain-sides, in the west; on the east, within a hundred yards under a slope, is Loch Beg. It is not a mile in circumference, and all but some eighty yards of shore is defended against the angler by wide beds of water-lilies, with their pretty white floating lamps, or by tall sedges and reeds. Nor is the wading easy. Four steps you make with safety, at the fifth your foremost leg sinks in mud apparently bottomless. Most people fish only the eastern side, whereof a few score yards are open, with a rocky and gravelly bottom.

Now, all lochs have their humours. In some trout like a big fly, in some a small one, but almost all do best with a rough wind or rain. I knew enough of Loch Beg to approach it at noon on a blazing day of sunshine, when the surface was like glass. It was like that when first I saw it, and a shepherd warned us that we "would dae naething"; we did little, indeed, but I rose nearly every rising fish I cast over, losing them all, too, and in some cases being broken, as I was using very fine gut, and the fish were heavy. Another trial seemed desirable, and the number of rising trout was most tempting. All over it trout were rising to the natural fly, with big circles like those you see in the Test at twilight; while in the centre, where no artificial fly can be cast for want of a boat, a big fish would throw himself out of the water in his eagerness. One such I saw which could not have weighed under three pounds, a short, thick, dark-yellow fish.

I was using a light two-handed rod, and fancied that a single Test-fly on very fine tackle would be the best lure. It certainly rose the trout, if one threw into the circle they made; but they never were hooked. One fish of about a pound and a half threw himself out of the water at it, hit it, and broke the fine tackle. So I went on raising them, but never getting them. As long as the sun blazed and no breeze ruffled the water, they rose bravely, but a cloud or even a ripple seemed to send them down.

At last I tried a big alder, and with that I actually touched a few, and even landed several on the shelving bank. Their average weight, as we proved on several occasions, was exactly three-quarters of a pound; but we never succeeded in landing any of the really big ones.

A local angler told me he had caught one of two pounds, and lost another "like a young grilse," after he had drawn it on to the bank. I can easily believe it, for in no loch, but one, have I ever seen so many really big and handsome fish feeding. Loch Beg is within a mile of a larger and famous loch, but it is infinitely better, though the other looks much more favourable in all ways for sport. The only place where fishing is easy, as I have said, is a mere strip of coast under the hill, where there is some gravel, and the mouth of a very tiny feeder, usually dry. Off this place the trout rose freely, but not near so freely as in a certain corner, quite out of reach without a boat, where the leviathans lived and sported.

After the little expanse of open shore had been fished over a few times, the trout there seemed to grow more shy, and there was a certain monotony in walking this tiny quarter-deck of space. So I went round to the west side, where the water-lilies are. Fish were rising about three yards beyond the weedy beds, and I foolishly thought I would try for them. Now, you cannot overestimate the difficulty of casting a fly across yards of water-lilies. You catch in the weeds as you lift your line for a fresh cast, and then you have to extricate it laboriously, shortening line, and then to let it out again, and probably come to grief once more.

I saw a trout rise, with a huge sullen circle dimpling round him, cast over him, raised him, and missed him. The water was perfectly still, and the "plop" made by these fish was very exciting and tantalising. The next that rose took the alder, and, of course, ran right into the broad band of lilies. I tried all the dodges I could think of, and all that Mr.

Halford suggests. I dragged at him hard. I gave him line. I sat down and endeavoured to disengage my thoughts, but I never got a glimpse of him, and finally had to wade as far in as I dared, and save as much of the casting line as I could; it was very little.

There was one thing to be said for the trout on this side: they meant business. They did not rise shyly, like the others, but went for the fly if it came at all near them, and then, down they rushed, and bolted into the lily-roots.

A new plan occurred to me. I put on about eighteen inches of the stoutest gut I had, to the end I knotted the biggest sea-trout fly I possessed, and, hooking the next fish that rose, I turned my back on the loch and ran uphill with the rod. Looking back I saw a trout well over a pound flying across the lilies; but alas! the hold was not strong enough, and he fell back. Again and again I tried this method, invariably hooking the trout, though the heavy short casting-line and the big fly fell very awkwardly in the dead stillness of the water. I had some exciting runs with them, for they came eagerly to the big fly, and did not miss it, as they had missed the Red Quill, or Whitchurch Dun, with which at first I tried to beguile them. One, of only the average weight, I did drag out over the lilies; the others fell off in mid-journey, but they never broke the uncompromising stout tackle.

With the first chill of evening they ceased rising,

and I left them, not ungrateful for their very peculiar manners and customs. The chances are that the trout beyond the band of weeds never see an artificial fly, and they are, therefore, the more guileless—at least, late in the season. In spring, I believe, the lilies are less in the way, and I fear some one has put a Berthon boat on the loch in April. But it is not so much what one catches in Loch Beg, as the monsters which one might catch that make the tarn so desirable.

The loch seems to prove that any hill-tarn might be made a good place for sport, if trout were introduced where they do not exist already. But the size of these in Loch Beg puzzles me, nor can one see how they breed, as breed they do: for twice or thrice I caught a fingerling, and threw him in again. No burn runs out of the loch, and, even in a flood, the feeder is so small, and its course so extremely steep, that one cannot imagine where the fish manage to spawn. The only loch known to me where the common trout are of equal size, is on the Border. It is extremely deep, with very clear water, and with scarce any spawning ground. On a summer evening the trout are occasionally caught; three weighing seven pounds were taken one night, a year or two ago. I have not tried the evening fishing, but at all other times of day have found them the "dourest" of trout, and they grow dourer. But one is always lured on by the spectacle of the monsters which throw themselves out of water, with a splash that echoes through all the circuit of the low green hills. They probably reach at least four or five pounds, but it is unlikely that the biggest take the fly, and one may doubt whether they propagate their species, as small trout are never seen there.

There are two ways of enlarging the size of trout which should be carefully avoided. Pike are supposed to keep down the population and leave more food for the survivors, minnows are supposed to be nourishing food. Both of these novelties are dangerous. Pike have been introduced in that long lovely sheet of water, Loch Ken, and I have never once seen the rise of a trout break that surface, so "hideously serene." Trout, in lochs which have become accustomed to feeding on minnows, are apt to disdain fly altogether. Of course there are lochs in which good trout coexist with minnows and with pike, but these inmates are too dangerous to be introduced. The introduction, too, of Loch Leven trout is often disappointing. Sometimes they escape down the burn into the river in floods; sometimes, perhaps for lack of proper food and sufficient, they dwindle terribly in size, and become no better than "brownies." In St. Mary's Loch, in Selkirkshire, some Canadian trout were introduced. Little or nothing has been seen of them, unless some small creatures of a quarter of a pound, extraordinarily silvery, and more often in the air than in the water when hooked, are these children of the remote

West. If they grew up, and retained their beauty and sprightliness, they would be excellent substitutes for sea-trout. Almost all experiments in stocking lochs have their perils, except the simple experiment of putting trout where there were no trout before. This can do no harm, and they may increase in weight, let us hope not in wisdom, like the curiously heavy and shy fish mentioned in the beginning of this paper.

LOCH LEVEN

~

I had a friend once, an angler, who in winter was fond of another sport. He liked to cast his louis into the green baize pond at Monte Carlo, and, on the whole, he was generally "broken." He seldom landed the golden fish of the old man's dream in Theocritus. When the croupier had gaffed all his money he would repent and say, "Now, that would have kept me at Loch Leven for a fortnight." One used to wonder whether a fortnight of Loch Leven was worth an afternoon of the pleasure of losing at Monte Carlo. The loch has a name for being cockneyfied, beset by whole fleets of competitive anglers from various angling clubs in Scotland. That men should competitively angle shows, indeed, a great want of true angling sentiment. To fish in a crowd is odious, to work hard for prizes of flasks and creels and fly-books is to mistake the true meaning of the pastime. However, in this crowded age men are so constituted that they like to turn a contemplative exercise into a kind of Bank Holiday. There is no use in arguing with such persons; the worst of their pleasure is that it tends to change a Scotch loch into something like the pond of the Welsh Harp, at Hendon. It is always good news to read in the papers how the Dundee Walton Society had a bad day, and how the first prize was won by Mr. Macneesh, with five trout weighing three pounds and three quarters. Loch Leven, then, is crowded and cockneyfied by competitions; it has also no great name for beauty of landscape. Every one to his own taste in natural beauty, but in this respect I think Loch Leven is better than its reputation. It is certainly more pictorial, so to speak, than some remote moor lochs up near Cape Wrath; Forsinard in particular, where the scenery looks like one gigantic series of brown "baps," flat Scotch scones, all of low elevation, all precisely similar to each other.

Loch Leven is not such a cockney place as the majority of men who have not visited it imagine. It really is larger than the Welsh Harp at Hendon, and the scenery, though not like that of Ben Cruachan or Ben Mohr, excels the landscape of Middlesex. At the northern end is a small town, grey, with some red roofs and one or two characteristic Fifeshire church-towers, squat and strong. There are also a few factory chimneys, which are not fair to outward view, nor appropriate by a loch-side. On the west are ranges of distant hills, low but not uncomely. On the east rises a beautiful moorland steep with broken and graceful outlines. When the sun shines on the red tilled land, in spring; when the smoke of burning gorse coils up all day long into the sky, as if the Great Spirit were taking his pipe of peace on the mountains; when the islands are mirrored on the glassy water, then the artist rejoices, though the angler knows that he will waste his day. As far as fishing goes, he is bound to be "clean," as the boatmen say—to catch nothing; but the solemn peace, and the walls and ruined towers of Queen Mary's prison, may partially console the fisher. The accommodation is agreeable, there is a pleasant inn—an old town-house, perhaps, of some great family, when the great families did not rush up to London, but spent their winters in such country towns as Dumfries and St. Andrews. The inn has a great green garden at its doors, and if the talk is mainly of fishing, and if every one tells of his monster trout that escaped the net, there is much worse conversation than that.

When you reach Kinross, and, after excellent ham and eggs, begin to make a start, the cockney element is most visible at the first. Everybody's name is registered in a book; each pays a considerable, but not exorbitant, fee for the society—often well worth the money—and the assistance of boatmen. These gentlemen are also well provided with luncheon and beer, and, on the whole, there is more pleasure in the life of a Loch Leven boatman than in most arts, crafts, or professions. He takes the rod when his patron is lazy; it is said that he often catches the trout;[1] he sees

---

1. Too true, alas!

a good deal of good company, and, if his basket be heavy, who so content as he? The first thing is to row out to a good bay, and which will prove a good bay depends on the strength and direction of the wind. Perhaps the best fishing is farthest off, at the end of a long row, but the best scenery is not so distant. A good deal hangs on an early start when there are many boats out.

Loch Leven is a rather shallow loch, seldom much over fifteen feet deep, save where a long narrow rent or geological flaw runs through the bottom. The water is of a queer glaucous green, olive-coloured, or rather like the tint made when you wash out a box of water-colour paints. This is not so pretty as the black wave of Loch Awe or Loch Shin, but has a redeeming quality in the richness of the feeding for trout. These are fabled to average about a pound, but are probably a trifle under that weight, on the whole. They are famous, and, according to Sir Walter Scott, were famous as long ago as in Queen Mary's time, for the bright silver of their sides, for their pink flesh, and gameness when hooked. Theorists have explained all this by saying that they are the descendants of land-locked salmon. The flies used on the loch are smaller than those favoured in the Highlands; they are sold attached to casts, and four flies are actually employed at once. Probably two are quite enough at a time. If a veteran trout is attracted by seeing four flies, all of different species, and these like nothing in nature, all conspiring to descend on him at once, he must be less cautious than we generally find him. The Hampshire angler, of course, will sneer at the whole proceeding, the "chucking and chancing it," in the queer-coloured wave, and the use of so many fanciful entomological specimens. But the Hampshire angler is very welcome to try his arts, in a calm, and his natural-looking cocked-up flies. He will probably be defeated by a grocer from Greenock, sinking his four flies very deep, as is, by some experts, recommended. The trout are capricious, perhaps as capricious as any known to the angler, but they are believed to prefer a strong east wind and a dark day. The east wind is nowhere, perhaps, so bad as people fancy; it is certainly not so bad as the north wind, and on Loch Leven it is the favourite. The man who is lucky enough to hit on the right day, and to land a couple of dozen Loch Leven trout, has very good reason to congratulate himself, and need envy nobody. But such days and such takes are rare, and the summer of 1890 was much more unfortunate than that of 1889.

One great mistake is made by the company which farms the Loch, stocks it, supplies the boats, and regulates the fishing. They permit trolling with angels, or phantoms, or the natural minnow. Now, trolling may be comparatively legitimate, when the boat is being pulled against the wind to its drift, but there is no more skill in it than in sitting in an omnibus. But for trolling, many a boat would come home "clean" in the evening, on days of calm, or when, for other reasons of their own, the trout refuse to take the artificial fly. Yet there are men at Loch Leven who troll all day, and poor sport it must be, as a trout of a pound or so has no chance on a trolling-rod. This method is inimical to fly-fishing, but is such a consolation to the inefficient angler that one can hardly expect to see it abolished. The unsuccessful clamour for trolling, instead of consoling themselves, as sportsmen should do, with the conversation of the gillies, their anecdotes of great trout, and their reminiscences of great anglers, especially of the late Mr. Russell, the famed editor of the "Scotsman." This humourist is gradually "winning his way to the mythical." All fishing stories are attached to him; his eloquence is said (in the language of the historian of the Buccaneers) to have been "florid"; he is reported to have thrown his fly-book into Loch Leven on an unlucky day, saying, "You brutes, take your choice," and a rock, which he once hooked and held on to, is named after him, on the Tweed. In addition to the humane and varied conversation of the boatmen, there is always the pure pleasure of simply gazing at the hillsides and at the islands. They are as much associated with the memory of Mary Stuart Hermitage or even Holyrood. On that island was her prison; here the rude Morton tried to bully her into signing away her rights; hence she may often have watched the shore at night for the lighting of a beacon, a sign that a rescue was at hand.

The hills, at least, are much as she may have seen them, and the square towers and crumbling walls on the island met her eyes when they were all too strong. The "quay" is no longer "rude," as when "The Abbot" was written, and is crowded with the green boats of the Loch Leven Company. But you still land on her island under "the huge old tree" which Scott saw, which the unhappy Mary may herself have seen. The small garden and the statues are gone, the garden whence Roland Graeme led Mary to the boat and to brief liberty and hope unfulfilled. Only a kind of ground-plan remains of the halls where Lindesay and Ruthven browbeat her forlorn Majesty. But you may climb the staircase where Roland Graeme stood sentinel, and feel a touch, of what Pepys felt when he kissed a dead Queen—Katherine of Valois. Like Roland Graeme, the Queen may have been "wearied to death of this Castle of Loch Leven," where, in spring, all seems so beautiful, the trees budding freshly above the yellow celandine and among the grey prison walls. It was a kindlier prison house than Fotheringay, and minds peaceful and contented would gladly have taken "this for a hermitage."

The Roman Emperors used to banish too

powerful subjects to the lovely isles that lie like lilies on the Ægean. Plutarch tried to console these exiles, by showing them how fortunate they were, far from the bustle of the Forum, the vices, the tortures, the noise and smoke of Rome, happy, if they chose, in their gardens, with the blue waters breaking on the rocks, and, as he is careful to add, *with plenty of fishing*. Mr. Mahaffy calls this "rhetorical consolation," and the exiles may have been of his mind. But the exiles would have been wise to listen to Plutarch, and, had I enjoyed the luck of Mary Stuart, when Loch Leven was not overfished, when the trout were uneducated, never would I have plunged into politics again. She might have been very happy, with Ronsard's latest poems, with Italian romances, with a boat on the loch, and some Rizzio to sing to her on the still summer days. From her Castle she would hear how the politicians were squabbling, lying, raising a man to divinity and stoning him next day, cutting each other's heads off, swearing and forswearing themselves, conspiring and caballing. *Suave mari*, and the peace of Loch Leven and the island hermitage would have been the sweeter for the din outside. A woman, a Queen, a Stuart, could not attain, and perhaps ought not to have attained, this epicureanism. Mary Stuart had her chance, and missed it; perhaps, after all, her shrewish female gaoler made the passionless life impossible.

These, at Loch Leven, are natural reflections.

The place has a charm of its own, especially if you make up your mind not to be disappointed, not to troll, and not to envy the more fortunate anglers who shout to you the number of their victories across the wave. Even at Loch Leven we may be contemplative, may be quiet, and go a-fishing.[2]

2. It should be added that large trout, up to six pounds, are sometimes taken. One boatman assured me that he had caught two three-pounders at one cast.

THE BLOODY DOCTOR
~

(A BAD DAY ON CLEARBURN)

Thou askest me, my brother, how first and where I met the Bloody Doctor? The tale is weird, so weird that to a soul less proved than thine I scarce dare speak of the adventure.

* * * * *

This, perhaps, would be the right way of beginning a story (not that it is a story exactly), with the title forced on me by the name and nature of the hero. But I do not think I could keep up the style without a lady-collaborator; besides, I have used the term "weird" twice already, and thus played away the trumps of modern picturesque diction. To return to our Doctor: many a bad day have I had on Clearburn Loch, and never a good one. But one thing draws me always to the loch when I have the luck to be within twenty miles of it. There are trout in Clearburn! The Border angler knows that the trout in his native waters is nearly as extinct as the dodo. Many causes have combined to extirpate the shy and spirited fish. First, there are too many anglers:

Twixt Holy Lee and Clovenfords,
A tentier bit ye canna hae,

sang that good old angler, now with God, Mr. Thomas Tod Stoddart. But between Holy Lee and Clovenfords you may see half a dozen rods on every pool and stream. There goes that leviathan, the angler from London, who has been beguiled hither by the artless "Guide" of Mr. Watson Lyall. There fishes the farmer's lad, and the schoolmaster, and the wandering weaver out of work or disinclined to work. In his rags, with his thin face and red "goatee" beard, with his hazel wand and his home-made reel, there is withal something kindly about this poor fellow, this true sportsman. He loves better to hear the lark sing than the mouse cheep; he wanders from depopulated stream to depopulated burn, and all is fish that comes to his fly. Fingerlings he keeps, and does not return to the water "as pitying their youth." Let us not grudge him his sport as long as he fishes fair, and he is always good company. But he, with all the other countless fishermen, make fish so rare and so wary that, except after a flood in Meggat or the Douglas burn, trout are scarce to be taken by ordinary skill. As for

Thae reiving cheils
Frae Galashiels,

who use nets, and salmon roe, and poisons, and dynamite, they are miscreants indeed; they spoil the sport, not of the rich, but of their own class, and of every man who would be quiet, and go angling in the sacred streams of Christopher North and the Shepherd. The mills, with their dyes and dirt, are also responsible for the dearth of trout.

> Untainted yet thy stream, fair Teviot, runs,

Leyden sang; but now the stream is very much tainted indeed below Hawick, like Tweed in too many places. Thus, for a dozen reasons, trout are nigh as rare as red deer. Clearburn alone remains full of unsophisticated fishes, and I have the less hesitation in revealing this, because I do not expect the wanderer who may read this page to be at all more successful than myself. No doubt they are sometimes to be had, by the basketful, but not often, nor by him who thinks twice before risking his life by smothering in a peaty bottom.

To reach Clearburn Loch, if you start from the Teviot, you must pass through much of Scott's country and most of Leyden's. I am credibly informed that persons of culture have forgotten John Leyden. He was a linguist and a poet, and the friend of Walter Scott, and knew

> The mind whose fearless frankness naught could move,
> The friendship, like an elder brother's love.

We remember what distant and what deadly shore has Leyden's cold remains, and people who do not know may not care to be reminded.

Leaving Teviot, with Leyden for a guide, you walk, or drive,

> Where Bortha hoarse, that loads the meads with sand,
> Rolls her red tide.

Not that it was red when we passed, but *electro purior*.

> Through slaty hills whose sides are shagged with thorn,
> Where springs, in scattered tufts, the dark green corn,
> Towers wood-girt Harden far above the vale.

And very dark green, almost blue, was the corn in September, 1888. Upwards, always upwards, goes the road till you reach the crest, and watch far below the wide champaign, like a sea, broken by the shapes of hills, Windburg and Eildon, and Priesthaughswire, and "the rough skirts of stormy Ruberslaw," and Penchrise, and the twin Maidens, shaped like the breasts of Helen. It is an old land, of war, of Otterburn, and Ancrum, and the Raid of the Fair Dodhead; but the plough has passed over all but the upper pastoral solitudes. Turning again to the downward slope you see the loch of Alemoor, small and sullen, with Alewater feeding it. Nobody knows much about the trout in it. "It is reckoned the residence of the water-cow," a monster like the Australian bunyip. There was a water-cow in Scott's loch of Cauldshiels, above Abbotsford. The water-cow has not lately emerged from Alemoor to attack the casual angler. You climb again by gentle slopes till you reach a most desolate tableland. Far beyond it is the round top of Whitecombe, which again looks down on St. Mary's Loch, and up the Moffat, and across the Meggat Water; but none of these are within the view. Round are *pastorum loca vasta*, lands of Buccleugh and Bellenden, Deloraine, Sinton, Headshaw, and Glack. Deloraine, by the way, is pronounced "Delorran," and perhaps is named from Orran, the Celtic saint. On the right lies, not far from the road, a grey sheet of water, and this is Clearburn, where first I met the Doctor.

The loch, to be plain, is almost unfishable. It is nearly round, and everywhere, except in a small segment on the eastern side, is begirt with reeds of great height. These reeds, again, grow in a peculiarly uncomfortable, quaggy bottom, which rises and falls, or rather which jumps and sinks when you step on it, like the seat of a very luxurious arm-chair. Moreover, the bottom is pierced with many springs, wherein if you set foot you shall have thrown your last cast.

By watching the loch when it is frozen, a man might come to learn something of the springs; but, even so, it is hard to keep clear of them in summer. Now the wind almost always blows from the west, dead against the little piece of gravelly shore at the eastern side, so that casting against it is hard work and unprofitable. On this day, by a rare chance, the wind blew from the east, though the sky at first was a brilliant blue, and the sun hot and fierce. I walked round to the east side, waded in, and caught two or three small fellows. It was slow work, when suddenly there began the greatest rise of trout I ever saw in my life. From the edge of the loch as far as one could clearly see across it there was that endless plashing murmur, of all sounds in this world the sweetest to the ear. Within the view of the eye, on each cast, there were a dozen trout rising all about, never leaping, but seriously and solemnly feeding. Now is my chance at last, I fancied; but it was not so—far from it. I might throw over the very noses of the beasts, but they seldom even glanced at the (artificial) fly. I tried them with Greenwell's Glory, with a March brown, with "the woodcock wing and hare-lug," but it was almost to no purpose. If one did raise a fish, he meant not business—all but "a casual brute," which broke the already weakened part of a small "glued-up" cane rod. I had to twist a piece of paper round the broken end, wet it, and push it into the joint, where it hung on somehow, but was not pleasant to cast with. From twelve to half-past one the gorging went merrily forward, and I saw what the fish were rising at. The whole surface of the loch, at least on the east side, was absolutely peppered with large, hideous insects. They had big grey-white wings, bodies black as night, and brilliant crimson legs, or feelers, or whatever naturalists call them. The trout seemed as if they could not have too much of these abominable wretches, and the flies were blown across the loch, not singly, but in populous groups. I had never seen anything like them in any hook-book, nor could I deceive the trout by the primitive dodge of tying a red thread round the shank of a dark fly. So I waded out, and fell to munching a frugal sandwich and watching Nature, not without a cigarette.

Now Nature is all very well. I have nothing to say against her of a Sunday, or when trout are not rising. But she was no comfort to me now. Smiling she gazed on my discomfiture. The lovely lines of the hills, curving about the loch, and with their deepest dip just opposite where I sat, were all of a golden autumn brown, except in the violet distance. The grass of Parnassus grew thick and white around me, with its moonlight tint of green in the veins. On a hillside by a brook the countryfolk were winning their hay, and their voices reached me softly from far off. On the loch the marsh-fowl flashed and dipped, the wild ducks played and dived and rose; first circling high and higher, then, marshalled in the shape of a V, they made for Alemoor. A solitary heron came quite near me, and tried his chance with the fish, but I think he had no luck. All this is pleasant to remember, and

I made rude sketches in the fly-leaves of a copy of Hogg's poems, where I kept my flies. But what joy was there in this while the "take" grew fainter and ceased at least near the shore? Out in the middle, where few flies managed to float, the trout were at it till dark. But near shore there was just one trout who never stopped gorging all day. He lived exactly opposite the nick in the distant hills, and exactly a yard farther out than I could throw a fly. He was a big one, and I am inclined to think that he was the Devil. For, if I had stepped in deeper, and the water had come over my wading boots, the odds are that my frail days on earth would have been ended by a chill, and I knew this, and yet that fish went on tempting me to my ruin. I suppose I tried to reach him a dozen times, and cast a hundred, but it was to no avail. At length, as the afternoon grew grey and chill, I pitched a rock at him, by way of showing that I saw through his fiendish guile, and I walked away.

There was no rise now, and the lake was leaden and gloomy. When I reached the edge of the deep reeds I tried, once or twice, to wade through them within casting distance of the water, but was always driven off by the traitorous quagginess of the soil. At last, taking my courage in both hands, I actually got so near that I could throw a fly over the top of the tall reeds, and then came a heavy splash, and the wretched little broken rod nearly doubled up. "Hooray, here I am among the big ones!" I said, and held on. It was now that I learned the nature of Nero's diversion when he was an angler in the Lake of Darkness. The loch really did deserve the term "grim"; the water here was black, the sky was ashen, the long green reeds closed cold about me, and beyond them there was trout that I could not deal with. For when he tired of running, which was soon, he was as far away as ever. Draw him through the forest of reeds I could not. At last I did the fatal thing. I took hold of the line, and then, "plop," as the poet said. He was off. A young sportsman on the bank who had joined me expressed his artless disappointment. I cast over the confounded reeds once more. "Splash!"—the old story! I stuck to the fish, and got him into the watery wood, and then he went where the lost trout go. No more came on, so I floundered a yard or two farther, and climbed into a wild-fowl's nest, a kind of platform of matted reeds, all yellow and faded. The nest immediately sank down deep into the water, but it stopped somewhere, and I made a cast. The black water boiled, and the trout went straight down and sulked. I merely held on, till at last it seemed "time for us to go," and by cautious tugging I got him through the reedy jungle, and "gruppit him," as the Shepherd would have said. He was simply but decently wrapped round, from snout to tail, in very fine water-weeds, as in a garment. Moreover, he was as black as your hat, quite unlike the comely yellow trout who live on the gravel in Clearburn. It hardly seemed sensible to get drowned in this gruesome kind of angling, so, leaving the Lake of Darkness, we made for Buccleugh, passing the cleugh where the buck was ta'en. Surely it is the deepest, the steepest, and the greenest cleugh that is shone on by the sun! Thereby we met an angler, an ancient man in hodden grey, strolling home from the Rankle burn. And we told him of our bad day, and asked him concerning that hideous fly, which had covered the loch and lured the trout from our decent Greenwells and March browns. And the ancient man listened to our description of the monster, and He said: "Hoot, ay; ye've jest forgathered wi' the Bloody Doctor."

This, it appears, is the Border angler's name for the horrible insect, so much appreciated by trout. So we drove home, when all the great tableland was touched with yellow light from a rift in the west, and all the broken hills looked blue against the silvery grey. God bless them! for man cannot spoil them, nor any revolution shape them other than they are. We see them as the folk from Flodden saw them, as Leyden knew them, as they looked to William of Deloraine, as they showed in the eyes of Wat of Harden and of Jamie Telfer of the Fair Dodhead. They have always girdled a land of warriors and of people fond of song, from the oldest ballad-maker to that Scotch Probationer who wrote,

> Lay me here, where I may see
> Teviot round his meadows flowing,
> And about and over me
> Winds and clouds for ever going.

It was dark before we splashed through the ford of Borthwick Water, and dined, and wrote to Mr. Anderson of Princes Street, Edinburgh, for a supply of Bloody Doctors. But we never had a chance to try them. I have since fished Clearburn from a boat, but it was not a day of rising fish, and no big ones came to the landing-net. There are plenty in the loch, but you need not make the weary journey; they are not for you nor me.

THE LADY OR THE SALMON?

~

The circumstances which attended and caused the death of the Hon. Houghton Grannom have not long been known to me, and it is only now that, by the decease of his father, Lord Whitchurch, and the extinction of his noble family, I am permitted to divulge the facts. That the true tale of my unhappy friend will touch different chords in different breasts, I am well aware. The sportsman, I think, will hesitate to approve him; the fair, I hope, will absolve. Who are we, to scrutinise human motives, and to award our blame to actions which, perhaps, might have been our own, had opportunity beset and temptation beguiled us? There is a certain point at which the keenest sense of honour, the most chivalrous affection and devotion, cannot bear the strain, but break like a salmon line under a masterful stress. That my friend succumbed, I admit; that he was his own judge, the severest, and passed and executed sentence on himself, I have now to show.

I shall never forget the shock with which I read in the "Scotsman," under "Angling," the following paragraph:

"Tweed.—Strange Death of an Angler.—An unfortunate event has cast a gloom over fishers in this district. As Mr. K---, the keeper on the B--- water, was busy angling yesterday, his attention was caught by some object floating on the stream. He cast his flies over it, and landed a soft felt hat, the ribbon stuck full of salmon-flies. Mr. K--- at once hurried up-stream, filled with the most lively apprehensions. These were soon justified. In a shallow, below the narrow, deep and dangerous rapids called 'The Trows,' Mr. K--- saw a salmon leaping in a very curious manner. On a closer examination, he found that the fish was attached to a line. About seventy yards higher he found, in shallow water, the body of a man, the hand still grasping in death the butt of the rod, to which the salmon was fast, all the line being run out. Mr. K--- at once rushed into the stream, and dragged out the body, in which he recognised with horror the Hon. Houghton Grannom, to whom the water was lately let. Life had been for some minutes extinct, and though Mr. K--- instantly hurried for Dr. ---, that gentleman could only attest the melancholy fact. The wading in 'The Trows' is extremely dangerous and difficult, and Mr. Grannom, who was fond of fishing without an attendant, must have lost his balance, slipped, and been dragged down by the weight of his waders. The recent breaking off of the hon. gentleman's contemplated marriage on the very wedding-day will be fresh in the memory of our readers."

This was the story which I read in the newspaper

during breakfast one morning in November. I was deeply grieved, rather than astonished, for I have often remonstrated with poor Grannom on the recklessness of his wading. It was with some surprise that I received, in the course of the day, a letter from him, in which he spoke only of indifferent matters, of the fishing which he had taken, and so forth. The letter was accompanied, however, by a parcel. Tearing off the outer cover, I found a sealed document addressed to me, with the superscription, "Not to be opened until after my father's decease." This injunction, of course, I have scrupulously obeyed. The death of Lord Whitchurch, the last of the Grannoms, now gives me liberty to publish my friend's *Apologia pro morte et vita sua.*

"Dear Smith" (the document begins), "Before you read this—long before, I hope—I shall have solved the great mystery—if, indeed, we solve it. If the water runs down to-morrow, and there is every prospect that it will do so, I must have the opportunity of making such an end as even malignity cannot suspect of being voluntary. There are plenty of fish in the water; if I hook one in 'The Trows,' I shall let myself go whither the current takes me. Life has for weeks been odious to me; for what is life without honour, without love, and coupled with shame and remorse? Repentance I cannot call the emotion which gnaws me at the heart, for in similar circumstances (unlikely as these are to occur) I feel that I would do the same thing again.

"Are we but automata, worked by springs, moved by the stronger impulse, and unable to choose for ourselves which impulse that shall be? Even now, in decreeing my own destruction, do I exercise free-will, or am I the sport of hereditary tendencies, of mistaken views of honour, of a seeming self-sacrifice, which, perhaps, is but selfishness in disguise? I blight my unfortunate father's old age; I destroy the last of an ancient house; but I remove from the path of Olive Dunne the shadow that must rest upon the sunshine of what will eventually, I trust, be a happy life, unvexed by memories of one who loved her passionately. Dear Olive! how pure, how ardent was my devotion to her none knows better than you. But Olive had, I will not say a fault, though I suffer from it, but a quality, or rather two qualities, which have completed my misery. Lightly as she floats on the stream of society, the most casual observer, and even the enamoured beholder, can see that Olive Dunne has great pride, and no sense of humour. Her dignity is her idol. What makes her, even for a moment, the possible theme of ridicule is in her eyes an unpardonable sin. This sin, I must with penitence confess, I did indeed commit. Another woman might have forgiven me. I know not how that may be; I throw myself on the mercy of the court. But, if another could pity and pardon, to Olive this was impossible. I have never seen her since that fatal moment when, paler than her orange blossoms, she swept through the porch of the church, while I, dishevelled, mud-stained, half-drowned—ah! that memory will torture me if memory at all remains. And yet, fool, maniac, that I was, I could not resist the wild, mad impulse to laugh which shook the rustic spectators, and which in my case was due, I trust, to hysterical but not unmanly emotion. If any woman, any bride, could forgive such an apparent but most unintentional insult, Olive Dunne, I knew, was not that woman. My abject letters of explanation, my appeals for mercy, were returned unopened. Her parents pitied me, perhaps had reasons for being on my side, but Olive was of marble. It is not only myself that she cannot pardon, she will never, I know, forgive herself while my existence reminds her of what she had to endure. When she receives the intelligence of my demise, no suspicion will occur to her; she will not say 'He is fitly punished;' but her peace of mind will gradually return.

"It is for this, mainly, that I sacrifice myself, but also because I cannot endure the dishonour of a laggard in love and a recreant bridegroom.

"So much for my motives: now to my tale.

"The day before our wedding-day had been the happiest in my life. Never had I felt so certain of Olive's affections, never so fortunate in my own. We parted in the soft moonlight; she, no doubt, to finish her nuptial preparations; I, to seek my couch in the little rural inn above the roaring waters of the Budon.[1]

> "Move eastward, happy earth, and leave
>   Yon orange sunset fading slow;
> From fringes of the faded eve
>   Oh, happy planet, eastward go,

I murmured, though the atmospheric conditions were not really those described by the poet.

> "Ah, bear me with thee, smoothly borne,
>   Dip forward under starry light,
> And move me to my marriage morn,
>   And round again to—

"'River in grand order, sir,' said the voice of Robins, the keeper, who recognised me in the moonlight. 'There's a regular monster in the Ashweil,' he added, naming a favourite cast; 'never saw nor heard of such a fish in the water before.'

"'Mr. Dick must catch him, Robins,' I answered; 'no fishing for me to-morrow.'

"'No, sir,' said Robins, affably. 'Wish you joy, sir, and Miss Olive, too. It's a pity, though! Master Dick, he throws a fine fly, but he gets flurried with a big fish, being young. And this one is a topper.'

"With that he gave me good-night, and I went to bed, but not to sleep. I was fevered with happiness; the past and future reeled before my wakeful vision.

---

1. From motives of delicacy I suppress the true name of the river.

I heard every clock strike; the sounds of morning were astir, and still I could not sleep. The ceremony, for reasons connected with our long journey to my father's place in Hampshire, was to be early—half-past ten was the hour. I looked at my watch; it was seven of the clock, and then I looked out of the window: it was a fine, soft grey morning, with a south wind tossing the yellowing boughs. I got up, dressed in a hasty way, and thought I would just take a look at the river. It was, indeed, in glorious order, lapping over the top of the sharp stone which we regarded as a measure of the due size of water.

"The morning was young, sleep was out of the question; I could not settle my mind to read. Why should I not take a farewell cast, alone, of course? I always disliked the attendance of a gillie. I took my salmon rod out of its case, rigged it up, and started for the stream, which flowed within a couple of hundred yards of my quarters. There it raced under the ash tree, a pale delicate brown, perhaps a little thing too coloured. I therefore put on a large Silver Doctor, and began steadily fishing down the ash-tree cast. What if I should wipe Dick's eye, I thought, when, just where the rough and smooth water meet, there boiled up a head and shoulders such as I had never seen on any fish. My heart leaped and stood still, but there came no sensation from the rod, and I finished the cast, my knees actually trembling beneath me. Then

I gently lifted the line, and very elaborately tested every link of the powerful casting-line. Then I gave him ten minutes by my watch; next, with unspeakable emotion, I stepped into the stream and repeated the cast. Just at the same spot he came up again; the huge rod bent like a switch, and the salmon rushed straight down the pool, as if he meant to make for the sea. I staggered on to dry land to follow him the easier, and dragged at my watch to time the fish; a quarter to eight. But the slim chain had broken, and the watch, as I hastily thrust it back, missed my pocket and fell into the water. There was no time to stoop for it; the fish started afresh, tore up the pool as fast as he had gone down it, and, rushing behind the torrent, into the eddy at the top, leaped clean out of the water. He was 70 lbs. if he was an ounce. Here he slackened a little, dropping back, and I got in some line. Now he sulked so intensely that I thought he had got the line round a rock. It might be broken, might be holding fast to a sunken stone, for aught that I could tell; and the time was passing, I knew not how rapidly. I tried all known methods, tugging at him, tapping the butt, and slackening line on him. At last the top of the rod was slightly agitated, and then, back flew the long line in my face. Gone! I reeled up with a sigh, but the line tightened again. He had made a sudden rush under my bank, but there he lay again like a stone. How long? Ah! I cannot tell how long! I heard the church clock strike, but missed the number of the strokes. Soon he started again down-stream into the shallows, leaping at the end of his rush—the monster. Then he came slowly up, and 'jiggered' savagely at the line. It seemed impossible that any tackle could stand these short violent jerks. Soon he showed signs of weakening. Once his huge silver side appeared for a moment near the surface, but he retreated to his old fastness. I was in a tremor of delight and despair. I should have thrown down my rod, and flown on the wings of love to Olive and the altar. But I hoped that there was time still—that it was not so very late! At length he was failing. I heard ten o'clock strike. He came up and lumbered on the surface of the pool. Gradually I drew him, plunging ponderously, to the gravelled beach, where I meant to 'tail' him. He yielded to the strain, he was in the shallows, the line was shortened. I stooped to seize him. The frayed and overworn gut broke at a knot, and with a loose roll he dropped back towards the deep. I sprang at him, stumbled, fell on him, struggled with him, but he slipped from my arms. In that moment I knew more than the anguish of Orpheus. Orpheus! Had I, too, lost my Eurydice? I rushed from the stream, up the steep bank, along to my rooms. I passed the church door. Olive, pale as her orange-blossoms, was issuing from the porch. The clock pointed to 10.45. I was ruined, I knew it, and I laughed. I laughed like a lost spirit. She swept past me, and, amidst the amazement of the gentle and simple, I sped wildly away. Ask me no more. The rest is silence."

* * * * *

Thus ends my hapless friend's narrative. I leave it to the judgment of women and of men. Ladies, would you have acted as Olive Dunne acted? Would pride, or pardon, or mirth have ridden sparkling in your eyes? Men, my brethren, would ye have deserted the salmon for the lady, or the lady for the salmon? I know what I would have done had I been fair Olive Dunne. What I would have done had I been Houghton Grannom I may not venture to divulge. For this narrative, then, as for another, "Let every man read it as he will, and every woman as the gods have given her wit."[2]

---

2. After this paper was in print, an angler was actually drowned while engaged in playing a salmon. This unfortunate circumstance followed, and did not suggest the composition of the story.

A Tweedside Sketch

~

The story of the following adventure—this deplorable confession, one may say—will not have been written in vain if it impresses on young minds the supreme necessity of carefulness about details. Let the "casual" and regardless who read it—the gatless, as they say in Suffolk—ponder the lesson which it teaches: a lesson which no amount of bitter experience has ever impressed on the unprincipled narrator. Never do anything carelessly whether in fishing or in golf, and carry this important maxim even into the most serious affairs of life. Many a battle has been lost, no doubt, by lack of ammunition, or by plenty of ammunition which did not happen to suit the guns; and many a salmon has been lost, ay, and many a trout, for want of carefulness, and through a culpable inattention to the soundness of your gut, and tackle generally. What fiend is it that prompts a man just to try a hopeless cast, in a low water, without testing his tackle? As sure as you do that, up comes the fish, and with his first dash breaks your casting line, and leaves you lamenting. This doctrine I preach, being my own "awful example." "Bad and careless little boy," my worthy master used to say at school; and he would have provoked a smile in other circumstances. But Mr.

Trotter, of the Edinburgh Academy, had something about him (he usually carried it in the tail-pocket of his coat) which inspired respect and discouraged ribaldry. Would that I had listened to Mr. Trotter; would that I had corrected, in early life, the happy-go-lucky disposition to scatter my Greek accents, as it were, with a pepper-caster, to fish with worn tackle, and, generally, to make free with the responsibilities of life and literature. It is too late to amend, but others may learn wisdom from this spectacle of deserved misfortune and absolute discomfiture.

I am not myself a salmon-fisher, though willing to try that art again, and though this is a tale of salmon. To myself the difference between angling for trout and angling for salmon is like the difference between a drawing of Lionardo's, in silver point, and a loaded landscape by MacGilp, R.A. Trout-fishing is all an idyll, all delicacy—that is, trout-fishing on the Test or on the Itchen. You wander by clear water, beneath gracious poplar-trees, unencumbered with anything but a slim rod of Messrs. Hardy's make, and a light toy-box of delicate flies. You need seldom wade, and the water is shallow, the bottom is of silver gravel. You need not search all day at random, but you select a rising trout, and endeavour to lay the floating fly delicately over him. If you part with him, there is always another feeding merrily:

Invenies alium si te hic fastidit.

It is like an excursion into Corot's country, it is rich in memories of Walton and Cotton: it is a dream of peace, and they bring you your tea by the riverside. In salmon-fishing, on the Tweed at least, all is different. The rod, at all events the rod which some one kindly lent me, is like a weaver's beam. The high heavy wading trousers and boots are even as the armour of the giant of Gath. You have to plunge waist deep, or deeper, into roaring torrents, and if the water be at all "drumly" you have not an idea where your next step may fall. It may be on a hidden rock, or on a round slippery boulder, or it may be into a deep "pot" or hole. The inexperienced angler staggers like a drunken man, is occasionally drowned, and more frequently is ducked. You have to cast painfully, with steep precipitous banks behind you, all overgrown with trees, with bracken, with bramble. It is a boy's work to disentangle the fly from the branches of ash and elm and pine. There is no delicacy, and there is a great deal of exertion in all this. You do not cast subtilely over a fish which you know is there, but you swish, swish, all across the current, with a strong reluctance to lift the line after each venture and try another. The small of the back aches, and it is literally in the sweat of your brow that you take your diversion. After all, there are many blank days, when the salmon will look at no fly, or when you encounter the *Salmo irritans*, who rises with every appearance of earnest good-will, but never touches the hook, or, if he does touch it, runs out a couple of yards of line, and vanishes for ever. What says the poet?

> There's an accommodating fish,
>   In pool or stream, by rock or pot,
> Who rises frequent as you wish,
>   At "Popham," "Parson," or "Jock Scott,"
> Or almost any fly you've got
>   In all the furred and feathered clans.
> You strike, but ah, you strike him not
>   He is the *Salmo irritans*!

It may be different in Norway or on the lower casts of the Tweed, as at Floors, or Makerstoun; but higher up the country, in Scott's own country, at Yair or Ashiesteil, there is often a terrible amount of fruitless work to be done. And I doubt if, except in throwing a very long line, and knowing the waters by old experience, there is very much skill in salmon-fishing. It is all an affair of muscle and patience. The choice of flies is almost a pure accident. Every one believes in the fly with which he has been successful. These strange combinations of blues, reds, golds, of tinsel and worsted, of feathers and fur, are purely fantastic articles. They are like nothing in nature, and are multiplied for the fanciful amusement of anglers. Nobody knows why salmon rise at them;

nobody knows why they will bite on one day and not on another, or rather, on many others. It is not even settled whether we should use a bright fly on a bright day, and a dark fly on a dark day, as Dr. Hamilton advises, or reverse the choice as others use. Muscles and patience, these, I repeat, are the only ingredients of ultimate success.

However, one does do at Rome as the Romans do, and fishes for salmon in Tweed when the nets are off in October, when the yellowing leaves begin to fall, and when that beautiful reach of wooded valley from Elibank to the meeting of Tweed and Ettrick is in the height of its autumnal charm. Why has Yarrow been so much more besung than Tweed, in spite of the greater stream's far greater and more varied loveliness? The fatal duel in the Dowie Dens of Yarrow and the lamented drowning of Willie there have given the stream its 'pastoral melancholy,' and engaged Wordsworth in the renown of the water. For the poetry of Tweed we have chiefly, after Scott, to thank Mr. Stoddart, its loyal minstrel. "Dearer than all these to me," he says about our other valleys, "is sylvan Tweed."

> Let ither anglers choose their ain,
> And ither waters tak' the lead
> O' Hieland streams we covet nane,
> But gie to us the bonny Tweed;
> And gie to us the cheerfu' burn,
> That steals into its valley fair,

> The streamlets that, at ilka turn,
>> Sae saftly meet and mingle there.

He kept his promise, given in the following verse:

> And I, when to breathe is a labour, and joy
> Forgets me, and life is no longer the boy,
> On the labouring staff, and the tremorous knee,
> Will wander, bright river, to thee!

Life is always "the boy" when one is beside the Tweed. Times change, and we change, for the worse. But the river changes little. Still he courses through the keen and narrow rocks beneath the bridge of Yair.

> From Yair, which hills so closely bind,
> Scarce can the Tweed his passage find,
> Though much he fret, and chafe, and toil,
> Till all his eddying currents boil.

Still the water loiters by the long boat-pool of Yair, as though loath to leave the drooping boughs of the elms. Still it courses with a deep eddy through the Elm Wheel, and ripples under Fernilea, where the author of the "Flowers of the Forest" lived in that now mouldering and roofless hall, with the peaked turrets. Still Neidpath is fair, Neidpath of the unhappy maid, and still we mark the tiny burn at Ashiesteil, how in November,

> Murmuring hoarse, and frequent seen,

Through bush and briar, no longer green,
An angry brook, it sweeps the glade,
Brawls over rock and wild cascade,
And foaming brown, with doubled speed,
Hurries its waters to the Tweed.

Still the old tower of Elibank is black and strong in ruin; Elibank, the home of that Muckle Mou'd Meg, who made Harden after all a better bride than he would have found in the hanging ash-tree of her father. These are unaltered, mainly, since Scott saw them last, and little altered is the homely house of Ashiesteil, where he had been so happy. And we, too, feel but little change among those scenes of long ago, those best-beloved haunts of boyhood, where we have had so many good days and bad, days of rising trout and success; days of failure, and even of half-drowning.

One cannot reproduce the charm of the strong river in pool and stream, of the steep rich bank that it rushes or lingers by, of the green and heathery hills beyond, or the bare slopes where the blue slate breaks through among the dark old thorn-trees, remnants of the forest. It is all homely and all haunted, and, if a Tweedside fisher might have his desire, he would sleep the long sleep in the little churchyard that lies lonely above the pool of Caddon-foot, and hard by Christopher North's favourite quarters at Clovenfords. However, while we are still on earth, Caddon-foot is more attractive for her long sweep of salmon-pool—the home of sea-trout too—than precisely for her kirk-yard. There will be time enough for that, and time it is to recur to the sad story of the big fish and the careless angler. It was about the first day of October, and we had enjoyed a "spate." Salmon-fishing is a mere child of the weather; with rain almost anybody may raise fish, without it all art is apt to be vain. We had been blessed with a spate. On Wednesday the Tweed had been roaring red from bank to bank. Salmon-fishing was wholly out of the question, and it is to be feared that the innumerable trout-fishers, busy on every eddy, were baiting with salmon roe, an illegal lure. On Thursday the red tinge had died out of the water, but only a very strong wader would have ventured in; others had a good chance, if they tried it, of being picked up at Berwick. Friday was the luckless day of my own failure and broken heart. The water was still very heavy and turbid, a frantic wind was lashing the woods, heaps of dead leaves floated down, and several sheaves of corn were drifted on the current. The long boat-pool at Yair, however, is sheltered by wooded banks, and it was possible enough to cast, in spite of the wind's fury. We had driven from a place about five miles distant, and we had not driven three hundred yards before I remembered that we had forgotten the landing-net. But, as I expected nothing, it did not seem worth while to go back for this indispensable implement. We reached the waterside, and found that the trout were feeding below the pendent branches of the trees and in the quiet, deep eddies of the long boat-pool. One cannot see rising trout without casting over them, in preference to labouring after salmon, so I put up a small rod and diverted myself from the bank. It was to little purpose. Tweed trout are now grown very shy and capricious; even a dry fly failed to do any execution worth mentioning. Conscience compelled me, as I had been sent out by kind hosts to fish for salmon, not to neglect my orders. The armour—the ponderous gear of the fisher—was put on with the enormous boots, and the gigantic rod was equipped. Then came the beginning of sorrows. We had left the books of salmon flies comfortably reposing at home. We had also forgotten the whiskey flask. Everything, in fact, except cigarettes, had been left behind. Unluckily, not quite everything: I had a trout fly-book, and therein lay just one large salmon fly, not a Tweed fly, but a lure that is used on the beautiful and hopeless waters of the distant Ken, in Galloway. It had brown wings, a dark body, and a piece of jungle-cock feather, and it was fastened to a sea-trout casting-line. Now, if I had possessed no salmon flies at all, I must either have sent back for some, or gone on innocently dallying with trout. But this one wretched fly lured me to my ruin. I saw that the casting-line had a link which seemed rather twisted. I tried it; but, in the spirit of Don Quixote with his helmet, I did not try it hard. I waded into the easiest-looking part of the pool, just above a huge tree that dropped its boughs to the water, and began casting, merely from a sense of duty. I had not cast a dozen times before there was a heavy, slow plunge in the stream, and a glimpse of purple and azure.

"That's him," cried a man who was trouting on the opposite bank. Doubtless it was "him," but he had not touched the hook. I believe the correct thing would have been to wait for half an hour, and then try the fish with a smaller fly. But I had no smaller fly, no other fly at all. I stepped back a few paces, and fished down again. In Major Traherne's work I have read that the heart leaps, or stands still, or otherwise betrays an uncomfortable interest, when one casts for the second time over a salmon which has risen. I cannot honestly say that I suffered from this tumultuous emotion. "He will not come again," I said, when there was a long heavy drag at the line, followed by a shrieking of the reel, as in Mr. William Black's novels. Let it be confessed that the first hooking of a salmon is an excitement unparalleled in trout-fishing. There have been anglers who, when the salmon was once on, handed him over to the gillie to play and land. One would like to act as gillie to those lordly amateurs. My own fish rushed down stream, where the big tree stands. I had no hope of landing him if he took that course, because one could neither pass the rod under the boughs, nor wade out beyond them. But he soon came back, while one took in line, and discussed his probable size with the trout-fisher opposite. His size, indeed! Nobody knows what it was, for when he had come up to the point whence he had started, he began a policy of violent short tugs—not "jiggering," as it is called, but plunging with all his weight on the line. I had clean forgotten the slimness of the tackle, and, as he was clearly well hooked, held him perhaps too hard. Only a very raw beginner likes to take hours over landing a fish. Perhaps I held him too tight: at all events, after a furious plunge, back came the line; the casting line had snapped at the top link.

There was no more to be said or done, except to hunt for another fly in the trout fly-book. Here there was no such thing, but a local spectator offered me a huge fly, more like a gaff, and equipped with a large iron eye for attaching the gut to. Withal I suspect this weapon was meant, not for fair fishing, but for "sniggling." Now "sniggling" is a form of cold-blooded poaching. In the open water, on the Ettrick, you may see half a dozen snigglers busy. They all wear high wading trousers; they are all armed with stiff salmon-rods and huge flies. They push the line and the top joints of the rod deep into the water, drag it along, and then bring the hook out with a jerk. Often it sticks in the side of a salmon, and in this most unfair and unsportsmanlike way the free sport of honest people is ruined, and fish are diminished in number. Now, the big fly *may* have been an honest character, but he was sadly like a rake-hook in disguise. He did not look as if an fish could fancy him. I, therefore, sent a messenger across the river to beg, buy, or borrow a fly at "The Nest." But this pretty cottage is no longer the home of the famous angling club, which has gone a mile or two up the water and builded for itself a new dwelling. My messenger came back with one small fatigued-looking fly, a Popham, I think, which had been lent by some one at a farmhouse. The water was so heavy that the small fly seemed useless; however, we fastened it on as a dropper, using the sniggler as the trail fly; so exhausted were our resources, that I had to cut a piece of gut off a minnow tackle and attach the small fly to that. The tiny gut loop of the fly was dreadfully frayed, and with a heavy heart I began fishing again. My friend on the opposite side called out that big fish were rising in the bend of the stream, so thither I went, stumbling over rocks, and casting with much difficulty, as the high overgrown banks permit no backward sweep of the line. You are obliged to cast by a kind of forward thrust of the arms, a knack not to be acquired in a moment. I splashed away awkwardly, but at last managed to make a straight, clean cast. There was a slight pull, such as a trout gives in mid-stream under water. I raised the point, and again the reel sang aloud and gleefully as the salmon rushed down the stream farther and faster than the first. It is a very pleasant thing to hook a salmon when you are all alone, as I was then—alone with yourself and the Goddess of Fishing. This salmon, just like the other, now came back, and instantly began the old tactics of heavy plunging tugs. But I knew the gut was sound this time, and as I fancied he had risen to the sniggler, I had no anxiety about the tackle holding. One more plunge, and back came the line as before. He was off. One could have sat down and gnawed the reel. What had gone wrong? Why, the brute had taken the old fly from the farmhouse and had snapped the loop that attaches the gut. The little loop was still on the fragment of minnow tackle which fastened it to the cast.

There was no more chance, for there were now no more flies, except a small "cobbery," a sea-trout fly from the Sound of Mull. It was time for us to go, with a heavy heart and a basket empty, except for two or three miserable trout. The loss of those two salmon, whether big or little fish, was not the whole misfortune. All the chances of the day were gone, and seldom have salmon risen so freely. I had not been casting long enough to smoke half a cigarette, when I hooked each of those fish. They rose at flies which were the exact opposites of each other in size, character, and colour. They were ready to rise at anything but the sniggler. And I had nothing to offer them, absolutely nothing bigger than a small red-spinner from the Test. On that day a fisher, not far off, hooked nine salmon and landed four of them, in one pool, I never had such a chance before; the heavy flood and high wind had made the salmon as "silly" as perch. One might have caught half a dozen of the great sturdy fellows, who make all trout, even sea-trout, seem despicable minnows. Next day I fished again in the same water, with a friend. I rose a fish, but did not hook it, and he landed a small one, five minutes after we started, and we only had one other rise all the rest of the day. Probably it was not dark and windy enough, but who can explain the caprices of salmon? The only certain thing is, that carelessness always brings misfortune; that if your tackle is weak fish will hook themselves on days, and in parts of the water, where you expected nothing, and then will go away with your fly and your casting-lines. Fortune never forgives. He who is lazy, and takes no trouble because he expects no fish, will always be meeting heart-breaking adventures. One should never make a hopeless or careless cast; bad luck lies in wait for that kind of performance. These are the experiences that embitter a man, as they embittered Dean Swift, who, old and ill, neglected and in Irish exile, still felt the pang of losing a great trout when he was a boy. What pleasure is there in landscape and tradition when such accidents befall you?

The sun upon the Weirdlaw hill,
In Ettrick's vale is sinking sweet.

There is a fire of autumn colour in the tufted woods that embosom Fernilea. "Bother the setting sun," we say, and the Maid of Neidpath, and the "Flowers of the Forest," and the memories of Scott at Ashiesteil, and of Muckle Mou'd Meg, at Elibank. These are filmy, shadowy pleasures of the fancy, these cannot minister to the mind of him who has been "broken" twice, who cannot resume the contest for want of ammunition, and who has not even brought the creature-comfort of a flask. Since that woful day I have lain on the bank and watched excellent anglers skilfully flogging the best of water, and that water full of fish, without hooking one. Salmon-fishing, then, is a matter of chance, or of plodding patience. They will rise on one day at almost any fly (but the sniggler), however ill-presented to them. On a dozen other days no fly and no skill will avail to tempt them. The salmon is a brainless brute and the grapes are sour!

If only the gut had held, this sketch would have ended with sentiment, and a sunset, and the music of Ettrick, the melody of Tweed. In the gloaming we'd be roaming homeward, telling, perhaps, the story of the ghost seen by Sir Walter Scott near Ashiesteil, or discussing the Roman treasure still buried near Oakwood Tower, under an inscribed stone which men saw fifty years ago. Or was it a treasure of Michael Scott's, who lived at Oakwood, says tradition? Let Harden dig for Harden's gear, it is not for me to give hints as to its whereabouts. After all that ill-luck, to be brief, one is not in the vein for legendary lore, nor memories of boyhood, nor poetry, nor sunsets. I do not believe that one ever thinks of the landscape or of anything else, while there is a chance for a fish, and no abundance of local romance can atone for an empty creel. Poetical fishers try to make people believe these fallacies; perhaps they impose on themselves; but if one would really enjoy landscape, one should leave, not only the fly-book and the landing-net, but the rod and reel at home. And so farewell to the dearest and fairest of all rivers that go on earth, fairer than Eurotas or Sicilian Anapus with its sea-trout; farewell—for who knows how long?—to the red-fringed Gleddis-wheel, the rock of the Righ-wheel, the rushing foam of the Gullets, the woodland banks of Caddon-foot.

> The valleys of England are wide,
>   Her rivers rejoice every one,
> In grace and in beauty they glide,
> And water-flowers float at their side,
>   As they gleam in the rays of the sun.
>
> But where are the speed and the spray—
>   The dark lakes that welter them forth,
> Tree and heath nodding over their way—
> The rock and the precipice grey,
>   That bind the wild streams of the North?

Well, both, are good, the streams of north and south, but he who has given his heart to the Tweed, as did Tyro, in Homer, to the Enipeus will never change his love.

P.S.—That Galloway fly—"The Butcher and Lang"—has been avenged. A copy of him, on the line of a friend, has proved deadly on the Tweed, killing, among other victims, a sea-trout of thirteen pounds.

THE DOUBLE ALIBI

~

G len Aline is probably the loneliest place in the lone moorlands of Western Galloway. The country is entirely pastoral, and I fancy that the very pasture is bad enough. Stretches of deer-grass and ling, rolling endlessly to the feet of Cairnsmure and the circle of the eastern hills, cannot be good feeding for the least Epicurean of sheep, and sheep do not care for the lank and sour herbage by the sides of the "lanes," as the half-stagnant, black, deep, and weedy burns are called in this part of the country. The scenery is not unattractive, but tourists never wander to these wastes where no inns are, and even the angler seldom visits them. Indeed, the fishing is not to be called good, and the "lanes," which "seep," as the Scotch say, through marshes and beneath low hillsides, are not such excellent company as the garrulous and brawling brooks of the Border or of the Highlands. As the lanes flow, however, from far-away lochs, it happens that large trout make their way into them—trout which, if hooked, offer a gallant resistance before they can be hauled over the weeds that usually line the watercourses.

Partly for the sake of trying this kind of angling, partly from a temporary distaste for the presence of men and women, partly for the purpose of finishing a work styled "A History of the Unexplained," I once spent a month in the solitudes of Glen Aline. I stayed at the house of a shepherd who, though not an unintelligent man was by no means possessed of the modern spirit. He and his brother swains had sturdily and successfully resisted an attempt made by the schoolmaster at a village some seven miles off to get a postal service in the glen more frequently than once a week. A post once a week was often enough for lucky people who did not get letters twice a year. It was not my shepherd, but another, who once came with his wife to the village, after a twelve miles' walk across the hills, to ask "what the day of the week was?" They had lost count, and the man had attended to his work on a day which the dame averred to be the Sabbath. He denied that it *was* the Sabbath, and I believe that it turned out to be a Tuesday. This little incident gives some idea of the delightful absence of population in Glen Aline. But no words can paint the utter loneliness, which could actually be felt—the empty moors, the empty sky. The heaps of stones by a burnside, here and there, showed that a cottage had once existed where now was no habitation. One such spot was rather to be shunned by the superstitious, for here, about 1698, a cottar family had been evicted by endless unaccountable disturbances in the house. Stones were thrown by invisible hands—

though occasionally, by the way, a white hand, with no apparent body attached to it, was viewed by the curious who came to the spot. Heavy objects of all sorts floated in the air; rappings and voices were heard; the end wall was pulled down by an unknown agency. The story is extant in a pious old pamphlet called "Sadducees Defeated," and a great deal more to the same effect—a masterpiece by the parish minister, signed and attested by the other ministers of the Glen Kens. The Edinburgh edition of the pamphlet is rare; the London edition may be procured without much difficulty.

The site of this ruined cottage, however, had no terrors for the neighbours, or rather for the neighbour, my shepherd. In fact, he seemed to have forgotten the legend till I reminded him of it, for I had come across the tale in my researches into the Unexplained. The shepherd and his family, indeed, were quite devoid of superstition, and in this respect very unlike the northern Highlanders. However, the fallen cottage had nothing to do with my own little adventure in Glen Aline, and I mention it merely as the most notable of the tiny ruins which attest the presence, in the past, of a larger population. One cannot marvel that the people "flitted" from the moors and morasses of Glen Aline into less melancholy neighbourhoods. The very sheep seemed scarcer here than elsewhere; grouse-disease had devastated the moors, sportsmen consequently did not visit them; and only a few barren pairs, with crow-picked skeletons of dead birds in the heather now and then, showed that the shootings had once perhaps been marketable. My shepherd's cottage was four miles from the little-travelled road to Dalmellington; long bad miles they were, across bog and heather. Consequently I seldom saw any face of man, except in or about the cottage. My work went on rapidly enough in such an undisturbed life. Empires might fall, parties might break like bursting shells, and banks might break also: I plodded on with my labour, and went a-fishing when the day promised well. There was a hill loch (Loch Nan) about five miles away, which I favoured a good deal. The trout were large and fair of flesh, and in proper weather they rose pretty freely, and could be taken by an angler wading from the shore. There was no boat. The wading, however, was difficult and dangerous, owing to the boggy nature of the bottom, which quaked like a quicksand in some places. The black water, never stirred by duck or moorhen, the dry rustling reeds, the noisome smell of decaying vegetable-matter when you stirred it up in wading, the occasional presence of a dead sheep by the sullen margin of the tarn, were all opposed to cheerfulness. Still, the fish were *there*, and the "lane," which sulkily glided from the loch towards the distant river, contained some monsters, which took worm after a flood. One misty morning, as I had just topped the low ridge from which the loch became visible, I saw a man fishing from my favourite bench. Never had I noticed a human being there before, and I was not well pleased to think that some emissary of Mr. Watson Lyall was making experiments in Loch Nan, and would describe it in "The Sportsman's Guide." The mist blew white and thick for a minute or two over the loch-side, as it often does at Loch Skene; so white and thick and sudden that the bewildered angler there is apt to lose his way, and fall over the precipice of the *Grey Mare's Tail*. When the curtain of cloud rose again, the loch was lonely: the angler had disappeared. I went on rejoicing, and made a pretty good basket, as the weather improved and grew warmer—a change which gives an appetite to trout in some hill lochs. Among the sands between the stones on the farther bank I found traces of the angler's footsteps; he was not a phantom, at all events, for phantoms do not wear heavily nailed boots, as he evidently did. The traces, which were soon lost, of course, inclined me to think that he had retreated up a narrow green burnside, with rather high banks, through which, in rainy weather, a small feeder fell into the loch. I guessed that he had been frightened away by the descent of the mist, which usually "puts down" the trout and prevents them from feeding. In that case his alarm was premature. I marched homewards, happy with the unaccustomed weight of my basket, the contents of which were a welcome change from the usual porridge and potatoes, tea (without milk), jam, and scones of the shepherd's table. But, as I reached the height above the loch on my westward path, and looked back to see if rising fish were dimpling the still waters, all flushed as they were with sunset, behold, there was the Other Man at work again!

I should have thought no more about him had I not twice afterwards seen him at a distance, fishing up a "lane" ahead of me, in the loneliest regions, and thereby, of course, spoiling my sport. I knew him by his peculiar stoop, which seemed not unfamiliar to me, and by his hat, which was of the clerical pattern once known, perhaps still known, as "a Bible-reader's"—a low, soft, slouched black felt. The second time that I found him thus anticipating me, I left off fishing and walked rather briskly towards him, to satisfy my curiosity, and ask the usual questions, "What sport?" and "What flies?" But as soon as he observed me coming he strode off across the heather. Uncourteous as it seems, I felt so inquisitive that I followed him. But he walked so rapidly, and was so manifestly anxious to shake me off, that I gave up the pursuit. Even if he were a poacher whose conscience smote him for using salmon-roe, I was not "my brother's keeper," nor anybody's keeper. He might "otter" the loch, but how could I prevent him?

It was no affair of mine, and yet—where had

I seen him before? His gait, his stoop, the carriage of his head, all seemed familiar—but a short-sighted man is accustomed to this kind of puzzle: he is always recognising the wrong person, when he does not fail to recognise the right one.

I am rather short-sighted, but science has its resources. Two or three days after my encounter with this very shy sportsman, I went again to Loch Nan. But this time I took with me a strong field-glass. As I neared the crest of the low heathery slope immediately above the loch, whence the water first comes into view, I lay down on the ground and crawled like a deer-stalker to the skyline.

Then I got out the glass and reconnoitred. There was my friend, sure enough; moreover, he was playing a very respectable trout. But he was fishing on the near side of the loch, and though I had quite a distinct view of his back, and indeed of all his attenuated form, I was as far as ever from recognising him, or guessing where, if anywhere, I had seen him before. I now determined to stalk him; but this was not too easy, as there is literally no cover on the hillside except a long march dyke of the usual loose stones, which ran down to the loch-side, and indeed three or four feet into the loch, reaching it at a short distance to the right of the angler. Behind this I skulked, in an eagerly undignified manner, and was just about to climb the wall unobserved, when two grouse got up, with their wild "cluck cluck" of alarm, and flew down past the angler and over the loch. He did not even look round, but jerked his line out of the water, reeled it up, and set off walking along the loch-side. He was making, no doubt, for the little glen up which I fancied that he must have retreated on the first occasion when saw him. I set off walking round the tarn on my own side—the left side—expecting to anticipate him, and that he must pass me on his way up the little burnside. But I had miscalculated the distance, or the pace. He was first at the burnside; and now I cast courtesy and everything but curiosity to the winds, and deliberately followed him. He was a few score of yards ahead of me, walking rapidly, when he suddenly climbed the burnside to the left, and was lost to my eyes for a few moments. I reached the place, ascended the steep green declivity and found myself on the open undulating moor, with no human being in sight!

The grass and heather were short. I saw no bush, no hollow, where he could by any possibility have hidden himself. Had he met a Boojum he could not have more "softly and suddenly vanished away."

I make no pretence of being more courageous than my neighbours, and, in this juncture, perhaps I was less so. The long days of loneliness in waste Glen Aline, and too many solitary cigarettes, had probably injured my nerve. So, when I suddenly heard a sigh and the half-smothered sound of a convulsive cough-hollow, if ever a cough was hollow—hard by me, at my side as it were, and yet could behold no man, nor any place where a man might conceal himself—nothing but moor and sky and tufts of rushes—then I turned away, and walked down the glen: not slowly. I shall not deny that I often looked over my shoulder as I went, and that, when I reached the loch, I did not angle without many a backward glance. Such an appearance and disappearance as this, I remembered, were in the experience of Sir Walter Scott. Lockhart does not tell the anecdote, which is in a little anonymous volume, "Recollections of Sir Walter Scott," published before Lockhart's book. Sir Walter reports that he was once riding across the moor to Ashiesteil, in the clear brown summer twilight, after sunset. He saw a man a little way ahead of him, but, just before he reached the spot, the man disappeared. Scott rode about and about, searching the low heather as I had done, but to no purpose. He rode on, and, glancing back, saw the same man at the same place. He turned his horse, galloped to the spot, and again—nothing! "Then," says Sir Walter, "neither the mare nor I cared to wait any longer." Neither had I cared to wait, and if there is any shame in the confession, on my head be it!

There came a week of blazing summer weather; tramping over moors to lochs like sheets of burnished steel was out of the question, and I worked at my book, which now was all but finished. At length I wrote THE

END, and "ô le bon ouff! que je poussais," as Flaubert says about one of his own laborious conclusions. The weather broke, we had a deluge, and then came a soft cloudy day, with a warm southern wind suggesting a final march on Loch Nan. I packed some scones and marmalade into my creel, filled my flask with whiskey, my cigarette-case with cigarettes, and started on the familiar track with the happiest anticipations. The Lone Fisher was quite out of my mind; the day was exhilarating—one of those true fishing-days when you feel the presence of the sun without seeing him. Still, I looked rather cautiously over the edge of the slope above the loch, and, by Jove! there he was, fishing the near side, and wading deep among the reeds! I did not stalk him this time, but set off running down the hillside behind him, as quickly as my basket, with its load of waders and boots, would permit. I was within forty yards of him, when he gave a wild stagger, tried to recover himself, failed, and, this time, disappeared in a perfectly legitimate and accountable manner. The treacherous peaty bottom had given way, and his floating hat, with a splash on the surface, and a few black bubbles, were all that testified to his existence. There was a broken old paling hard by; I tore off a long plank, waded in as near as I dared, and, by help of the plank, after a good deal of slipping, which involved an exemplary drenching, I succeeded in getting him on to dry land. He was a distressing spectacle—his body and face all blackened with the slimy peat-mud; and he fell half-fainting on the grass, convulsed by a terrible cough. My first care was to give him whiskey, by perhaps a mistaken impulse of humanity; my next, as he lay, exhausted, was to bring water in my hat, and remove the black mud from his face.

Then I saw Percy Allen—Allen of St. Jude's! His face was wasted, his thin long beard (he had not worn a beard of old), clogged as it was with peat-stains, showed flecks of grey.

"Allen—Percy!" I said; "what wind blew you here?"

But he did not answer; and, as he coughed, it was too plain that the shock of his accident had broken some vessel in the lungs. I tended him as well as I knew how to do it. I sat beside him, giving him what comfort I might, and all the time my memory flew back to college days, and to our strange and most unhappy last meeting, and his subsequent inevitable disgrace. Far away from here—Loch Nan and the vacant moors—my memory wandered.

It was at Blocksby's auction-room, in a street near the Strand, on the eve of a great book-sale three years before, that we had met, for almost the last time, as I believed, though it is true that we had not spoken on that occasion. It is necessary that I should explain what occurred, or what I and three other credible witnesses believed to have occurred; for, upon my word, the more I see and hear of human evidence of any event, the less do I regard it as establishing anything better than an excessively probable hypothesis.

To make a long story as short as may be, I should say that Allen and I had been acquainted when we were undergraduates; that, when fellows of our respective colleges, our acquaintance had become intimate; that we had once shared a little bit of fishing on the Test; and that we were both book-collectors. I was a comparatively sane bibliomaniac, but to Allen the time came when he grudged every penny that he did not spend on rare books, and when he actually gave up his share of the water we used to take together, that his contribution to the rent might go for rare editions and bindings. After this deplorable change of character we naturally saw each other less, but we were still friendly. I went up to town to scribble; Allen stayed on at Oxford. One day I chanced to go into Blocksby's rooms; it was a Friday, I remember—there was to be a great sale on the Monday. There I met Allen in ecstasies over one of the books displayed in the little side room on the right hand of the sale-room. He had taken out of a glass case and was gloating over a book which, it seems, had long been the Blue Rose of his fancy as a collector. He was crazed about Longepierre, the old French amateur, whose volumes, you may remember, were always bound in blue morocco, and tooled, on the centre and at the corners, with his badge, the Golden Fleece. Now the tome which so fascinated Allen was a Theocritus, published at Rome by Caliergus—a Theocritus on blue paper, if you please, bound in Longepierre's morocco livery, *doublé* with red morocco, and, oh ecstasy! with a copy of Longepierre's version of one Idyll on the flyleaf, signed with the translator's initials, and headed "*à Mon Roy.*" It is known to the curious that Louis XIV. particularly admired and praised this little poem, calling it "a model of honourable gallantry." Clearly the grateful author had presented his own copy to the king; and here it was, when king and crown had gone down into dust.

Allen showed me the book; he could hardly let it leave his hands.

"Here is a pearl," he had said, "a gem beyond price!"

"I'm afraid you'll find it so," I said; "that is for a Paillet or Rothschild, not for you, my boy."

"I fear so," he had answered; "if I were to sell my whole library to-morrow, I could hardly raise the money;" for he was poor, and it was rumoured that his mania had already made him acquainted with the Jews.

We parted. I went home to chambers; Allen stayed adoring the unexampled Longepierre. That night I dined out, and happened to sit next a young lady who possessed a great deal of taste, though that was the least of her charms. The fashion for book-collecting was among her innocent pleasures; she had seen Allen's books at Oxford, and I told her of his longings for the Theocritus. Miss Breton at once was eager to see the book, and the other books, and I obtained leave to go with her and Mrs. Breton to the auction-rooms next day. The little side-room where the treasures were displayed was empty, except for an attendant, when we went in; we looked at the things and made learned remarks, but I admit that I was more concerned to look at Miss Breton than at any work in leather by Derome or Bauzonnet. We were thus a good deal occupied, perhaps, with each other; people came and went, while our heads were bent over a case of volumes under the window. When we did leave, on the appeal of Mrs. Breton, we both—both I and Kate—Miss Breton, I mean—saw Allen—at least I saw him, and believed she did—absorbed in gazing at the Longepierre Theocritus. He held it rather near his face; the gas, which had been lit, fell on the shining Golden Fleeces of the cover, on his long thin hands and eager studious features. It would have been a pity to disturb him in his ecstasy. I looked at Miss Breton; we both smiled, and, of course, I presumed we smiled for the same reason.

I happen to know, and unluckily did it happen, the very minute of the hour when we left Blocksby's. It was a quarter to four o'clock—a church-tower was chiming the three-quarters in the Strand, and I looked half mechanically at my own watch, which was five minutes fast. On Sunday I went down to Oxford, and happened to walk into Allen's rooms. He was lying on a sofa reading the "Spectator." After chatting a little, I said, "You took no notice of me, nor of the Bretons yesterday, Allen, at Blocksby's."

"I didn't see you," he said; and as he was speaking there came a knock at the door.

"Come in!" cried Allen, and a man entered who was a stranger to me. You would not have called him a gentleman perhaps. However, I admit that I am possibly no great judge of a gentleman.

Allen looked up.

"Hullo, Mr. Thomas," he said, "have you come up to see Mr. Mortby?" mentioning a well-known Oxford bibliophile. "Wharton," he went on, addressing me, "this is Mr. Thomas from Blocksby's." I bowed. Mr. Thomas seemed embarrassed. "Can I have a word alone with you, sir?" he murmured to Allen.

"Certainly," answered Allen, looking rather surprised. "You'll excuse me a moment, Wharton," he said to me. "Stop and lunch, won't you? There's the old 'Spectator' for you;" and he led Mr. Thomas into a small den where he used to hear his pupils read their essays, and so forth.

In a few minutes he came out, looking rather pale, and took an embarrassed farewell of Mr. Thomas.

"Look here, Wharton," he said to me, "here is a curious business. That fellow from Blocksby's tells me that the Longepierre Theocritus disappeared yesterday afternoon; that I was the last person in whose hand it was seen, and that not only the man who always attends in the room but Lord Tarras and Mr. Wentworth, saw it in my hands just before it was missed."

"What a nuisance!" I answered. "You were looking at it when Miss Breton and I saw you, and you didn't notice us; Does Thomas know *when*—I mean about what o'clock—the book was first missed?"

"That's the lucky part of the whole worry," said Allen. "I left the rooms at three exactly, and it was missed about ten minutes to four; dozens of people must have handled it in that interval of time. So interesting a book!"

"But," I said, and paused—"are you sure your watch was right?"

"Quite certain; besides, I looked at a church clock. Why on earth do you ask?"

"Because—I am awfully sorry—there is some unlucky muddle; but it was exactly a quarter, or perhaps seventeen minutes, to four when both Miss Breton and I saw you absorbed in the Longepierre."

"Oh, it's quite *impossible*," Allen answered; "I was far enough away from Blocksby's at a quarter to four."

"That's all right," I said. "Of course you can prove that; if it is necessary; though I dare say the book has fallen behind a row of others, and has been found by this time. Where were you at a quarter to four?"

"I really don't feel obliged to stand a cross-examination before my time," answered Allen, flushing a little. Then I remembered that I was engaged to lunch at All Souls', which was true enough; convenient too, for I do not quite see how the conversation could have been carried on pleasantly much further. For I *had* seen him—not a doubt about it. But there was one curious thing. Next time I met Miss Breton I told her the story, and said, "You remember how we saw Allen, at Blocksby's, just as we were going away?"

"No," she said, "I did not see him; where was he?"

"Then why did you smile—don't you remember? I looked at him and at you, and I thought you smiled!"

"Because—well, I suppose because *you* smiled," she said. And the subject of the conversation was changed.

It was an excessively awkward affair. It did not come "before the public," except, of course, in the agreeably mythical gossip of an evening paper. There was no more public scandal than *that*. Allen was merely ruined. The matter was introduced to the notice of the Wardens and the other Fellows of St.

Jude's. What Lord Tarras saw, what Mr. Wentworth saw, what *I* saw, clearly proved that Allen was in the auction-rooms, and had the confounded book in his hand, at an hour when, as *he* asserted, he had left the place for some time. It was admitted by one of the people employed at the sale-rooms that Allen had been noticed (he was well known there) leaving the house at three. But he must have come back again, of course, as at least four people could have sworn to his presence in the show-room at a quarter to four o'clock. When he was asked in a private interview, by the Head of his College, to say where he went after leaving Blocksby's Allen refused to answer. He merely said that he could not prove the facts; that his own word would not be taken against that of so many unprejudiced and even friendly witnesses. He simply threw up the game. He resigned his fellowship; he took his name off the books; he disappeared.

There was a good deal of talk; people spoke about the unscrupulousness of collectors, and repeated old anecdotes on that subject. Then the business was forgotten. Next, in a year's time or so, the book—the confounded Longepierre's Theocritus—was found in a pawnbroker's shop. The history of its adventures was traced beyond a shadow of doubt. It had been very adroitly stolen, and disposed of, by a notorious book-thief, a gentleman by birth—now dead, but well remembered. Ask Mr. Quaritch!

Allen's absolute innocence was thus demonstrated beyond cavil, though nobody paid any particular attention to the demonstration. As for Allen, he had vanished; he was heard of no more.

He was *here*; dying here, beside the black wave of lone Loch Nan.

All this, so long in the telling, I had time enough to think over, as I sat and watched him, and wiped his lips with water from the burn, clearer and sweeter than the water of the loch.

At last his fit of coughing ceased, and a kind of peace came into his face.

"Allen, my dear old boy," I said—I don't often use the language of affection—"did you never hear that all that stupid story was cleared up; that everyone knows you are innocent?"

He only shook his head; he did not dare to speak, but he looked happier, and he put his hand in mine.

I sat holding his hand, stroking it. I don't know how long I sat there; I had put my coat and waterproof under him. He was "wet through," of course; there was little use in what I did. What could I do with him? how bring him to a warm and dry place?

The idea seemed to strike him, for he half rose and pointed to the little burnside, across the loch. A plan occurred to me; I tore a leaf from my sketch-book, put the paper with pencil in his hand, and said,

"Where do you live? Don't speak. Write."

He wrote in a faint scrawl, "Help me to that burnside. Then I can guide you."

I hardly know how I got him there, for, light as he was, I am no Hercules. However, with many a rest, we reached the little dell; and then I carried him up its green side, and laid him on the heather of the moor.

He wrote again:

"Go to that clump of rushes—the third from the little hillock. Then look, but be careful. Then lift the big grass tussock."

The spot which Allen indicated was on the side of a rather steep grassy slope. I approached it, dragged at the tussock of grass, which came away easily enough, and revealed the entrance to no more romantic hiding-place than an old secret whiskey "still." Private stills, not uncommon in Sutherland and some other northern shires, are extinct in Galloway. Allen had probably found this one by accident in his wanderings, and in his half-insane bitterness against mankind had made it, for some time at least, his home. The smoke-blackened walls, the recesses where the worm-tub and the still now stood, all plainly enough betrayed the original user of the hiding-place. There was a low bedstead, a shelf or two, whereon lay a few books—a Shakespeare, a Homer, a Walton, Plutarch's "Lives"; very little else out of a library once so rich. There was a tub of oatmeal, a heap of dry peat, two or three eggs in a plate, some bottles, a keg of whiskey, some sardine-tins, a box with clothes—that was nearly all the "plenishing" of this hermitage. It was never likely to be discovered, except by the smoke, when the inmate lit a fire. The local shepherd knew it, of course, but Allen had bought his silence, not that there were many neighbours for the shepherd to tattle with.

Allen had recovered strength enough by this time to reach his den with little assistance. He made me beat up the white of one of the eggs with a little turpentine, which was probably, under the circumstances, the best styptic for his malady within his reach. I lit his fire of peats, undressed him, put him to bed, and made him as comfortable as might be in the den which he had chosen. Then I went back to the shepherd's, sent a messenger to the nearest doctor, and procured a kind of sledge, generally used for dragging peat home, wherein, with abundance of blankets for covering, I hoped to bring Allen back to the shepherd's cottage.

Not to delay over details, this was managed at last, and the unhappy fellow was under a substantial roof. But he was very ill; he became delirious and raved of many things—talked of old college adventures, bid recklessly for imaginary books, and practised other eccentricities of fever.

When his fever left him he was able to converse in a way—I talking, and he scrawling faintly with a pencil on paper. I told him how his character had been cleared, how he had been hunted for, advertised for, vainly enough. To the shepherds' cottages where he had lived till the beginning of that summer, newspapers rarely came; to his den in the old secret still, of course they never came at all.

His own story of what he had been doing at the fatal hour when so many people saw him at the auction-rooms was brief.

He had left the rooms, as he said, at three o'clock, pondering how he might raise money for the book on which his heart was set. His feet had taken him, half unconsciously, to

a dismal court,
Place of Israelite resort,

where dwelt and dealt one Isaacs, from whom he had, at various times, borrowed money on usury. The name of Isaacs was over a bell, one of many at the door, and, when the bell was rung, the street door "opened of his own accord," like that of the little tobacco-and-talk club which used to exist in an alley off Pall Mall. Allen rang the bell, the outer door opened, and, as he was standing at the door of Isaacs' chambers, before he had knocked, *that* portal also opened, and the office-boy, a young Jew, slunk cautiously out. On seeing Allen, he had seemed at once surprised and alarmed. Allen asked if his master was in; the lad answered "No" in a hesitating way; but on second thoughts, averred that Isaacs "would be back immediately," and requested Allen to go in and wait. He did so, but Isaacs never came, and Allen fell asleep. He had a very distinct and singular dream, he said, of being in Messrs. Blocksy's rooms, of handling the Longepierre, and of seeing Wentworth there, and Lord Tarras. When he wakened he was very cold, and, of course, it was pitch dark. He did not remember where he was; he lit a match and a candle on the chimney-piece. Then slowly his memory came back to him, and not only his memory, but his consciousness of what he had wholly forgotten—namely, that this was Saturday, the Sabbath of the Jews, and that there was not the faintest chance of Isaacs' arrival at his place of business. In the same moment the embarrassment and confusion of the young Israelite flashed vividly across his mind, and he saw that he was in a very awkward position. If that fair Hebrew boy had been robbing, or trying to rob, the till, then Allen's position was serious indeed, as here he was, alone, at an untimely hour, in the office. So he blew the candle out, and went down the dingy stairs as quietly as possible, took the first cab he met, drove to Paddington, and went up to Oxford.

It is probable that the young child of Israel, if he had been attempting any mischief, did not succeed in it. Had there been any trouble, it is likely enough that he would have involved Allen in the grief. Then

Allen would have been in a, perhaps, unprecedented position. He could have established an *alibi*, as far as the Jew's affairs went, by proving that he had been at Blocksby's at the hour when the boy would truthfully have sworn that he had let him into Isaacs' chambers. And, as far as the charge against him at Blocksby's went, the evidence of the young Jew would have gone to prove that he was at Isaacs', where he had no business to be, when we saw him at Blocksby's. But, unhappily, each *alibi* would have been almost equally compromising. The difficulty never arose, but the reason why Allen refused to give any account of what he had been doing, and where he had been, at four o'clock on that Saturday afternoon—a refusal that told so heavily against him—is now sufficiently clear. His statement would, we may believe, never have been corroborated by the youthful Hebrew, who certainly had his own excellent reasons for silence, and who probably had carefully established an alibi of his own elsewhere.

The true account of Allen's appearance, or apparition, at Blocksby's, when I and Tarras, Wentworth and the attendant recognised him, and Miss Breton did *not*, is thus part of the History of the Unexplained. Allen might have appealed to precedents in the annals of the Psychical Society, where they exist in scores, and are technically styled "collective hallucinations." But neither a jury, nor a judge, perhaps, would accept the testimony of experts in Psychical Research if offered in a criminal trial, nor acquit a wraith.

Possibly this scepticism has never yet injured the cause of an innocent man. Yet I know, in my own personal experience, and have heard from others, from men of age, sagacity, and acquaintance with the greatest affairs, instances in which people have been distinctly seen by sane, healthy, and honourable witnesses, in places and circumstances where it was (as we say) "physically impossible" that they should have been, and where they certainly were not themselves aware of having been. That is why human testimony seems to me to establish no more, in certain circumstances, than a highly probable working hypothesis—a hypothesis on which, of course, we are bound to act.

There is little more to tell. By dint of careful nursing, poor Allen was enabled to travel; he reached Mentone, and there the mistral ended him. He was a lonely man, with no kinsfolk; his character was cleared among the people who knew him best; the others have forgotten him. Nobody can be injured by this explanation of his silence when called on to prove his innocence, and of his unusually successful vanishing from a society which had never tried very hard to discover him in his retreat. He has lived and suffered and died, and left behind him little but an incident in the History of the Unexplained.

Editor's Afterword

~

Andrew Lang was born in Selkirk in the Scottish Borders in 1844. He was educated at St. Andrews University and at Balliol College, Oxford. A prolific writer, he distinguished himself across a vast array of disciplines – from history to anthropology, classical studies and poetry, literary criticism and biography – and held a lifelong sporting passion for fly-fishing.

Angling Sketches was first published in 1891. It rapidly went out of print and into a second edition. Lang added a new chapter for an 1895 edition called 'The Complete Bungler', a comic micro-drama between two fly-fishermen, one from Scotland and one from England. In miniature the two protagonists enact the single most pressing debate to ripple through the fly-fishing community in the last decades of the nineteenth century, and through much of the twentieth: whether one fished 'dry fly' versus 'wet fly', or 'upstream' versus 'down'. Lang belonged decidedly to the North and his little book of tales can be read as his defence of the northern, 'north-country' wet-fly tradition. But it is, of course, so much more.

By his own testimony Andrew Lang was not a great fisherman. A reader approaching his *Angling*

Sketches in the hope of finding snippets of fishing insight will be disappointed. Its inspiration lies elsewhere, for Lang was a consummate storyteller, and *Angling Sketches* is as much about spinning yarns as it is about spinning reels. Lang's insatiable narrative drive enlivens these delightful tales of adventure.

In essence fly-fishing has changed very little over the years. *Angling Sketches*, with its rich and intimate evocation of the lochs and rivers of Andrew Lang's youth, scattered throughout Lowland Scotland, speaks to us today in a voice as fresh and as entertaining as when it first appeared in 1891.

George Messo

R·H·B
Sporting Classics
Series

No. 1
The Book of the Grayling - T. E. Pritt

No. 2
Angling Sketches - Andrew Lang

No. 3
Chats on Angling - H. V. Hart-Davis

No. 4
The Teesdale Angler - R. Lakeland

Visit www.rhbks.com

www.ingramcontent.com/pod-product-compliance
Lightning Source LLC
Chambersburg PA
CBHW032003040426
42448CB00006B/471